THE · BUSINESS · SIDE · OF · GENERAL · PRACTICE

Making Sense of the NHS Complaints and Disciplinary Procedures

Edited by

DAVID PICKERSGILL

and

TONY STANTON

Foreword by

SIR DONALD IRVINE
President of the General Medical Council

RADCLIFFE ME[

D0676058

Radcliffe Medical Press Ltd
18 Marcham Road, Abingdon, Oxon OX14 1AA, UK

Radcliffe Medical Press, Inc.
141 Fifth Avenue, New York, NY 10010, USA

British Library Cataloguing-in-Publication Data

A catalogue record for this book is available from the British Library.

ISBN 1 85775 163 9

Library of Congress Cataloging-in-Publication Data is available.

Typeset by Acorn Bookwork, Salisbury
Printed and bound by Biddles Ltd, Guildford and King's Lynn

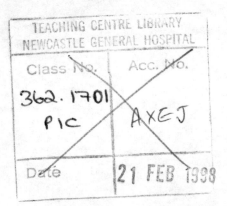

Contents

List of Contributors

JANE HANNA, *Law Fellow of Harris Manchester College, University of Oxford*

GERARD PANTING, *Head of UK Medical Services, Medical Protection Society*

DAVID PICKERSGILL, *General Practitioner, Member of the General Medical Services Committee, Chairman of the Statutes and Regulations Committee, Member of the British Medical Association Council, Chairman of the Complaints Working Party of the British Medical Association*

PETER SCHÜTTE, *Deputy Head of Advisory Services, The Medical Defence Union Ltd*

TONY STANTON, *Secretary, London Local Medical Committees, former Deputy Chairman, General Medical Services Committee, British Medical Association*

ANTHONY TOWNSEND, *Head of Conduct, General Medical Council*

Foreword

The publication of this book is both timely and welcome. Patients and doctors are having their first experience of the new NHS complaints and disciplinary procedures which are designed to be effective, efficient and fair to all concerned. It is essential that all general practitioners know broadly how the system works. As important, at least one partner in each practice should have a thorough understanding so that, if there is a complaint, the partnership knows exactly what to do and what the implications are.

This book does everything that is needed – and more. It covers the subject comprehensively. All chapters are written in a straightforward, accessible and eminently readable style which makes a heavy subject come alive. General practitioners and registrars should find it an invaluable addition to the practice library.

There is a further reason why its appearance now is so timely. Patients today are seeking better protection from poorly performing doctors. To this end the GMC's fitness to practise arrangements are being strengthened by the new performance procedures which come into operation in September 1997. The early recognition of dysfunctional doctors, adequate public protection, and the chance of effective remediation before damage is done to patients or the doctor with a problem, is critically dependent on sound local self-regulation in which doctors know what their duties and responsibilities are, and how to make the system work. Readers of this book will receive an invaluable grounding in key aspects of our new approach to professional self-regulation.

The writers are to be congratulated. The book deserves to be read widely.

Sir Donald Irvine
February 1997

Preface

'*A complaint is an expression of dissatisfaction which requires a response.*' (From *Practice Based Complaints Procedures*, NHSE 1996.)

'*Complaints are jewels to be treasured.*' (Secretary of State for Health 1995.)

It is a fact of life that anyone providing a service to the public will from time to time receive complaints about the way in which the service has been provided or about the outcome of a particular incident. Given the millions of contacts between patients and the NHS each year it is perhaps surprising that there are so few complaints. However, it is important that there should be in place a properly structured, easily accessible and readily understood mechanism to investigate those complaints and to provide the complainants with a clear explanation of what has happened. Where appropriate the system should enable an apology to be offered.

For many years the NHS complaints procedure was a complex, poorly understood and poorly operated process which often left those lodging the complaint and those being complained against feeling very dissatisfied, both with the process and the outcome. Continued pressure for reform both from patients' organizations and from representatives of the various health care professions led to the establishment of the Wilson Committee in 1993 which was charged with the responsibility of undertaking a review of the NHS complaints procedures and making recommendations for change. Following publication of their report and further public consultation, legislation was introduced in April 1996 which put into place a new complaints mechanism in the NHS.

This book sets out to explain the new processes in detail with particular reference to their implications for general practitioners, but also includes reference to the procedures in the hospital service where they differ from those in the family practitioner services and where they have relevance to general practitioners.

Given the responsibilities which the new procedures place on general practitioners for operating the initial stages of the complaints process, and given the increasingly litigious and complaint-minded society in which we live, we believe it is important that every person working in the health care field should have a full and clear understanding of the complaints procedures and thus be able to respond helpfully and positively in the event of receiving a complaint. We hope that this book will help to provide such an understanding.

David Pickersgill
Tony Stanton
February 1997

Acknowledgements

We would like to thank Jane Hanna, Anthony Townsend, Peter Schütte and Gerard Panting for their contributions to this book, and Sir Donald Irvine for writing the foreword.

We would also like to thank our secretaries, Gillian Kemp, Sally Dennis and Elaine Osborne for their patience and help in typing and collating the manuscript.

Our thanks also go to the staff at Radcliffe Medical Press who have encouraged us to write this book and to our many colleagues on the General Medical Services Committee of the British Medical Association who worked with us to prepare our evidence to the review of the NHS complaints procedure and supported us during the negotiations leading up to the introduction of the new procedures.

We would like to extend our special thanks to Samantha Jones of the GMSC Secretariat for her enormous contribution during the discussions and negotiations which led up to the implementation of the new complaints procedures.

1   The Old System – Why Change?

Tony Stanton

The Independent Review of the National Health Service (NHS) complaints procedures under the Chairmanship of Professor Alan Wilson, announced by the Secretary of State for Health in June 1993, was given the following terms of reference: 'To *review the procedures for the making and handling of complaints by NHS patients and their families in the United Kingdom, and the costs and benefits of alternatives to current procedures, and to make recommendations to the Secretary of State for Health and other Ministers'*.

The British Medical Association (BMA) was already concerned about complaints procedures relating to doctors and had previously set up a working group to consider proposals and initiatives in the field of NHS complaints. The report of the working group, which was approved by the Association's Council in September 1993, was then submitted to the Wilson Committee as the Association's evidence.

The BMA was well aware of discontent among patients and clinicians about many aspects of the complaints system. Many patients found the old system to be slow, impenetrable, unwieldy and failing to address their concerns. Doctors themselves recognized those shortcomings and found the system equally unhelpful. With more and more complaints being made, many of which were found to be unfounded or a result of misunderstandings, together with some which were clearly activated by malice, there was increasing stress on doctors.

The Wilson Committee's remit was very much to do with complaints about NHS services. It was not concerned with the much more complex field of litigation for medical negligence and compensation. The BMA's policy of supporting no-fault compensation for medical negligence has not yet found favour with legislators. There have subsequently been proposals from Lord Woolf about the streamlining of claims and procedures in respect of medical negligence.

Fundamental to the BMA's evidence was to establish the crucial point that any complaints procedure had to be seen to be fair. The purpose of a fair complaints procedure must be to investigate what happened during a consultation or procedure which had given rise to the complaint. The almost inevitable entanglement of a clinical complaints procedure with disciplinary action against a doctor was a potent cause of frustration both to patients and doctors, leading only to the dissatisfaction of all concerned. The BMA was therefore very keen to see that wherever practicable, complaints should be addressed in the first instance directly to the clinician concerned, without prejudice to using more formal systems if that approach proved unsuccessful. Only if a satisfactory explanation was not received should formal procedures be initiated.

The BMA therefore supported the view of the Consumers' Association that a good NHS complaints procedure should be: *'Visible, accessible, transparent, fast, impartial, effective, flexible with the right to appeal and effective monitoring. The primary function of the procedure should be to address the concerns of the complainant. It should, therefore, establish at an early stage what outcome the complainant is seeking'.*

In its evidence to the Wilson Committee the BMA dealt with each of these important points in turn.

- Visibility – There needed to be wider provision of easily available information about complaints procedures in hospitals, GPs' surgeries and community health clinics.

- Accessibility – There should be a single point of entry for all NHS complaints, whether hospital or general practice based. This needed to be locally sited.

- Transparency – Patients needed a report of the investigation of a complaint, although it was recognized that there was room for potential conflict as any such reports could be used as a basis for litigation.

- Speed was felt to be of the essence, with a strong recommendation that time limits for the completion of each stage by those running the complaints system should be built into it.

- Impartiality – Although perceived by many patients as being compromised by the involvement of doctors sitting in judgement on their colleagues, the perception of many doctors is that often members of the profession are more critical of their conduct than are lay members of panels.

- Effectiveness was likely to be enhanced in the view of the BMA by the new General Medical Council (GMC) Performance Review procedures and by encouraging a change of culture so that complaints can be acknowledged and used in a beneficial way to improve systems.

- Flexibility – As opposed to the treadmill of formal complaints procedures, the BMA highlighted the need for improved communication.

- The right to appeal is fundamental to the concept of natural justice, both for the patient and the doctor.

- Effective monitoring was firmly supported by the BMA, together with the need for the collection and an early publication of statistics about complaints on a National level.

In considering these issues, the BMA went on to recommend a new 'one door' system in which all complaints could be channelled initially through a single body, while retaining systems which reflected the different contractual status of different sectors of the profession. Given the need for expertise, training and for impartiality the BMA argued for a complaints unit to be established at regional level with a number of local, easily accessible offices sited at population centres or hospitals throughout the region. The local office would quickly assess all complaints and determine how they should be dealt with in consultation with a complainant to clarify their expectations, where necessary.

A powerful argument in favour of such a unit would be its complete independence of hospital management, individual health authority or indeed individual practices. It would be able to deal with complaints against not only the actions of doctors and other health professionals but also those against the provision of NHS services – effectively about the management of the NHS and the standard of its services. It would deal with complaints relating to all providers of NHS care and would ensure that universal standards were consistently applied across the board. In effect these local complaints offices would be organized as branches of an independent health authority and would have the power to deal with complaints relating to contractual and clinical matters. The Complaints Authority would need access to appropriate professional advice. It would receive information about the outcome of all complaints and action taken and would publish regular reports containing this information. The Complaints Authority would be responsible for ensuring that all aspects of NHS complaints procedures were well advertised locally, liaising with health authorities, NHS trusts, individual GPs, CHCs and bodies such as the Citizens' Advice Bureau, to ensure that this was done.

The BMA went on to argue that the local complaints offices would perform their role in the framework of a three-stage complaints procedure, with the following structure.

- Stage 1 – In-house informal procedures. In order to facilitate the resolution of many concerns and misunderstandings at the informal stage the BMA strongly endorsed the development of in-house informal procedures, in general practice, in hospital practice and for doctors working in public health medicine and community health.

- Stage 2 was seen as being an opportunity for conciliation, reinvestigation and explanation. It would come into play if a complainant was not satisfied at the informal stage. The proposal was that complaints would then move to a second stage at which the complaints office would consider what course of action to take.

- Stage 3, with its formal procedures, would come into play when neither Stage 1 nor Stage 2 had resolved the issue. In general practice, complaints concerning contractual or administrative matters would be dealt with by a formal Service Committee procedure administered by a regional grouping of the then family health service authorities (FHSAs). The BMA also proposed that a clinical complaints system similar to the current Stage 3 procedure for hospital consultants be developed. Complaints of a purely clinical nature would then be referred to an independent professional review conducted by two practising general practitioners from a regional panel. In hospital practice Stage 3 of the current clinical complaints procedure would be retained, and for doctors in public health medicine and community health a procedure similar to those for hospital practice should be developed.

The action following a Stage 3 investigation would be that in each case the Chief Executive of the trust or health authority would write formally to the complainant. In respect of contractual complaints, the BMA envisaged that the Chief Executive of the FHSA would decide on the basis of the Service Committee findings whether remedial or punitive action was necessary, and if so, what.

In summary, therefore, it was the BMA's view that complaints made against those working in the NHS should be dealt with by investigating what had happened, through the consideration of written and oral evidence, by a panel of impartial individuals with appropriate experience. The existing GP complaints system was felt to have become increasingly adversarial in nature, serving the interests of neither complainant nor doctor. The basic purpose of a Service Committee investigation, being an inquiry to establish the facts of a case, was in danger of being seen more as a trial. This raised serious questions, not least the evidential burden and standards of proof, the civil standard of proof requiring decisions on disputed evidence to reflect the balance of probability. The more serious the consequences, the more compelling must be the evidence required to tip the balance of probability and the BMA therefore did not recommend any alteration to standards of proof.

The experience of the Association was that financial withholdings from the GPs found in breach of their Terms of Service during the Service Committee procedure did not act as any form of deterrent. Furthermore, as evidence in such cases is not given on oath it was felt to be inappropriate for fines to be imposed in this way. There was therefore a very strong case for removing any disciplinary element from the investigative procedure, and financial withholdings should be abolished.

Better remedies for doctors against whom a complaint had been upheld might include:

- instructions to amend the practice or to comply with the Terms of Service

- a requirement to undertake appropriate post-graduate training

- referral to the GMC

- referral to the NHS Tribunal

- referral to hospital disciplinary procedures.

As with all other aspects of the complaints procedures, NHS tribunals which can determine whether or not a doctor should continue to work in the NHS, should conclude their business much more quickly, arguably with suspension on protected income for those doctors complaints against whom are of sufficient seriousness to warrant investigation by a tribunal.

The GMC exists primarily to protect the public and the BMA therefore supports the GMC's performance review procedures. The working group expressed the hope that an improved complaints investigation system will lead to more appropriate referrals to the GMC.

The general thrust of the BMA's policy being to encourage conciliation, explanation and where necessary apology, any increased involvement of lawyers in the complaints process was felt would hinder rather than help.

In conclusion the BMA welcomed the Secretary of State's review of NHS complaints procedures and recognized many of the general concerns expressed by other interested organizations about the shortcomings of the then current procedures and the need for a review to resolve the lack of information and delays in resolving complaints. It stressed the need for any new system to be fair to both the users of NHS services and professionals working within the health service and to remove those factors from the present system which caused unnecessary stress to be placed on doctors who are the subject of complaints. It wanted a non-adversarial, informal and speedy system for investigating complaints, and a mechanism for enabling doctors to obtain some redress against vexatious patients.

Fundamental to the review was that any new system should identify the precise matter of concern to the patient, to investigate it and provide an explanation and, where appropriate, an apology. Both doctors and the NHS as a whole needed to learn from complaints and take steps to ensure that methods of working or clinical practice were changed when that was shown to be necessary. The system needed to focus not just on the alleged actions of individuals but should be used as a means of addressing the shortcomings of the NHS as an organization.

2 The Wilson Report – 'Being Heard'

David Pickersgill

In mid-1993 the then Secretary of State for Health invited Professor Alan Wilson, Vice Chancellor of the University of Leeds, to Chair a Review Committee on NHS complaints procedures. The Committee included members drawn from a wide range of backgrounds, both within and outside the NHS and included among its membership a general practitioner with extensive experience of the old Service Committee and Tribunal arrangements. The report of the Committee was published in May 1994, some months later than had originally been anticipated, and it contained a very comprehensive review of the existing systems, comparisons of those systems with other organizations' and countries' complaints systems, and detailed the desirable features of effective procedures. It contained 67 recommendations, among the most important of which was a list of general principles which should be incorporated into any new NHS complaints procedure:

- responsiveness
- quality enhancement
- cost-effectiveness
- accessibility
- impartiality
- simplicity
- speed
- confidentiality
- accountability.

The report reminded readers that although the Patient's Charter had included the right to have complaints about NHS services investigated and for complainants to receive a full and prompt written reply, the central elements of the existing NHS complaints procedures were all designed before the health service reforms were introduced. Many of the procedures had remained largely unchanged since they had been introduced decades ago.

The Report stressed the need to satisfy complainants and suggested that the NHS needs effective complaints procedures so that complainants can be given a response to their complaints which aims to provide that satisfaction. Professor Wilson and his colleagues believed that such a system would avoid protracted correspondence and unnecessary litigation. They also believed that such effective responses would maintain and enhance the reputation of both individuals and organizations within the NHS and could enable the relationship between a patient and a practitioner to be restored. Importantly they also recognized that any complaints procedure must be seen by both practitioners and staff to be fair.

Analysis of existing procedures

The National Association of Health Authorities and Trusts (NAHAT) in its evidence to Wilson stated: *'the arrangements are seen as being over complex, failing to be user friendly, taking too long, often over defensive and often failing to give any satisfactory explanation of the conclusion reached'*. It was widely acknowledged by many parties who gave evidence to the Wilson Committee that complainants faced an uphill struggle when using the old NHS complaints procedures. At least nine different procedures for investigating complaints were identified in the Report. The procedures were often seen to be ineffective in meeting complainants' objectives. In many instances the actual handling of the complaint left much to be desired and some of the evidence received by the Wilson Committee suggested that the initial response of some complaints officers was poor or even hostile.

Whilst in some parts of the country the old informal conciliation procedures worked well, there was wide variation in their application and in their effectiveness. The formal Service Committee procedures had few friends, either among the public or within the profession. The Medical Defence Union (MDU) commented that: *'complainants appear to find the procedure lengthy, cumbersome and over regulated, and understandably they cannot relate the substance of their complaint to the narrower considerations of the Terms of Service imposed by the Regulations'*. The Health Service Ombudsman stated: *'the procedure is an amalgam of Terms of Service and complaints procedures, resulting in confusion and misunderstanding, and the promotion of an adversarial approach'*. The annual conference of Local Medical Committees, in a series of motions stretching back over several years, expressed their dissatisfaction with the old system and called for one which was less threatening, speedier and would provide for the investigation of complaints as a distinct process from any subsequent disciplinary action.

The Report compared the old complaints systems with those of other organizations and those in existence in other countries. It identified that in the private sector the two main aims of complaint handling seemed to be shared broadly, namely:

1 *'to satisfy those who complain, turning them from being potentially dissatisfied into satisfied customers or service users*

2 *to generate management information about aspects of the organization's service or products which cause customers' problems, to enable these problems to be addressed and levels of customer service improved'.*

The Report believes that the NHS can learn many lessons from the private sector, although it acknowledges that patients, unlike customers in the private sector, may not have any choice as to who provides their health care needs. Among the list of lessons which can be learnt from the private sector, the Report includes the following.

- Complainants do want an apology even if the company/organization was not at fault. This does not mean accepting responsibility for the problem.

- Complainants want a speedy response.

- Complainants want a reassurance that the company is taking the matter seriously, and will try to prevent a recurrence.

- Complainants do not want to be told:

  (a) that the rules were being followed so the organization was right all along

  (b) that they made a mistake so it is their own fault

  (c) detailed explanations of why a problem arose which come across as an excuse for poor services.

- It should be an objective to resolve as many complaints as possible at the first point of contact.

- Staff training on customer contact handling, defusing anger, and telephone techniques, and empowerment of front-line staff to satisfy complainants, all improve satisfaction.

In reviewing the arrangements in other countries, the Wilson Committee found a wide variety of practices, ranging from almost non-existent procedures to very formal complaints units established by national departments of health. At the time the Report was being written several countries were in the process of preparing legislation for the introduction of new health complaints procedures. In several instances these placed the responsibility for the initial investigation and explanation on the shoulders of the clinician about whom the complaint is being made.

The key principles in the Wilson Report recommendations

Responsiveness

Complaints procedures should be responsive and should aim to satisfy complainants. The Report acknowledges that this does not mean that all complainants will be satisfied with the outcome of their complaint, but the procedure should be directed to satisfying their objectives as well as those of the NHS.

Quality enhancement

Management information gained from the investigation of complaints can help to identify problems and sometimes suggest solutions. Improvements made as a result of these findings may lead to changes which can be to the benefit of all patients, and of those involved in providing services for the NHS.

Cost-effectiveness

The old systems were extremely costly to operate and the costs increased substantially the more formally complaints were investigated. It is self-evident that procedures must be cost-effective to operate. They must be capable of implementation within available resources.

Accessibility

Procedures must be well publicized and understandable to all and recognize the needs of vulnerable groups, such as children, people with mental health problems and people with learning difficulties, as well as reducing potential barriers of class, race, language and literacy.

Impartiality

Both the complainant and the respondent doctor have a right to expect a complaint to be investigated impartially. Equal support should be available to both parties to a complaint and everyone involved should feel that they have been treated fairly.

Simplicity

A simple complaints procedure is desirable and the Wilson Report suggested that there should be a common procedure for complaints arising in any part of the health service so that it is readily accessible for complainants and easier to use by those operating it.

Speed

The Report recommends that complainants should receive as fast a response as is possible without jeopardizing other principles. The Committee was unable to come to a unanimous agreement on the important issue of time limits for lodging complaints. In the end it recommended that the health departments examine the desirability of time limits for making complaints in the light of the arguments which it outlined in its report. However, it did recommend that the information given out about complaints procedures should encourage people to make complaints known as soon as possible after they become aware of a problem. It also made specific recommendations about the deadlines for responding to complaints.

Confidentiality

The Report emphasizes the need for complaints systems to abide by the general NHS duty of confidence in order that people may feel able to complain without fear that their current or future care will be compromised.

Accountability

This final principle makes it quite clear that chairmen and non-executive members of trusts are to be held ultimately responsible for the operation of their complaints systems and that responsibility is taken at the most senior level for the operation of complaints procedures.

Recommendations

In addition to incorporating the above principles in any new system, Professor Wilson and his colleagues recommended that there should be a common system for investigating complaints by NHS patients and that complaints, wherever they are lodged, are directed without delay to the appropriate person so that the complainant will receive a full response. The Report recommended unequivocally that complaints procedures should be concerned only with resolving complaints and not with disciplining practitioners or staff. The health departments were invited to re-examine the existing disciplinary procedures, particularly those for family practitioners.

The need for adequate simple and readily available written information was stressed, as well as the need for those handling complaints to make early personal contact with complainants in order to give a rapid, often oral, initial response. There are recommendations on the importance of training for all those involved in handling complaints and on the need for support for both complainants and respondents. There is recognition in the recommendations that not all complaints require a detailed and lengthy investigation. The degree of response should be appropriate to the seriousness of the complaint and also take into account the complainant's required degree of response. There is also recognition of the importance of an effective conciliation mechanism being more widely available throughout the NHS and that such conciliators should receive appropriate training.

Wilson suggested that the investigation of complaints should be split into two stages. The Stage 1 procedures would have three parts:

- an immediate first-line response

- second, investigation and/or conciliation and

- third, action by an officer of the FHSA which might include obtaining independent advice or establishing an independent inquiry.

The Stage 2 procedures would be for those complaints which were not adequately dealt with under Stage 1 procedures. Complaints would initially be screened and then considered by a panel of three members with the ability to appoint two additional members where there were issues of professional judgement or the requirement for specialist knowledge. The panels would be required to produce their final report within 40 working days and that report should be sent not only to the parties to the complaint, but also to the relevant Chief Executive who would judge what management action, if any, should follow.

Finally, the Report made two recommendations which required Parliamentary legislation in order to be introduced. The first was that the Health Service Ombudsman should have his jurisdiction extended to include GPs and matters relating to clinical judgement. The second was that the introduction of 'in-house' procedures in every general practice should become a Terms of Service requirement for general practitioners.

In producing its Report, the Wilson Committee received over 250 written submissions from various organizations and individuals, including of course, submissions from the major medical and patients' organizations. In addition numerous groups, including the British Medical Association, were invited to present 'oral evidence'. There was a surprising degree of unanimity in the submissions made, both by patients' organizations and medical organizations.

After the Report was published the Government invited responses from the public before setting out its own final response in a document entitled *Acting on Complaints*.

Following this further consultation process the new NHS complaints procedures were introduced on 1 April 1996. They incorporated most of the Wilson proposals. Broadly they involved the Stage 1 procedures – now called Local Resolution – and for GPs this requires each practice to have its own in-house procedure. An independent review procedure was also introduced for those cases which were not resolved by the local resolution process or were not considered suitable for dealing with in that manner. The introduction of these new methods of complaints investigation meant that any disciplinary process became an entirely separate matter and removed from patients the right to request that disciplinary action be taken against the doctor. The various processes including details of the new disciplinary procedures are discussed in greater depth in later chapters of this book.

3 In-house Complaints Procedures – Local Resolution

Tony Stanton

We are all consumers. The society in which we live is a consumer-orien-tated market. For the first 40 years of its existence, the NHS was often perceived as operating like a centrally organized, State-run monopoly. People who were unhappy with the service they received found that any criticisms they voiced tended to be met by a 'take it or leave it' attitude. With the separation of the purchasing and providing arms of the NHS, the substantially autonomous NHS trusts, and the widespread promulga-tion of Patient's Charters, the climate of complaints has changed irretrie-vably. General practice is, of course, not isolated from this and GPs are rightly proud of their independent contractor status. Whether they are practising as sole practitioners or in partnership with others, GPs are operating independent businesses. All businesses receive complaints, and sensible businesses find that their commercial success is enhanced, and not diminished, by encouraging their customers to express any dissatisfaction directly to the business itself and preferably as soon as possible once a cause for complaint comes to light.

Over recent years, many general practices have found it very useful to make such a cultural change. With the new complaints procedures, it is now obligatory to have practice-based procedures. These need to be effective, and must be seen to be fair. Just as in commercial life where unhappy customers have access to trading standards officers, professional associations, registration bodies and the courts, patients can also take complaints to health authorities, the ombudsman, the General Medical Council and the law. None of these alternatives is likely to prove a happy experience for the doctor at the centre of the complaint.

Since complaints are often intensely personal, either towards an indivi-dual GP or a particular member of staff, it is quite understandable that those on the receiving end feel very suspicious about the whole process. Ninety per cent of patient contacts with the NHS are through general practice and while those delivering patient care may not yet see complaints as 'jewels to be treasured', those complaints are undeniably one of the major growth points of the NHS. Complaints cannot be avoided, but they can be managed.

The Terms of Service require GPs to have a practice-based complaints procedure which complies with nationally agreed criteria. The criteria include three key elements:

- information
- investigation
- response.

Information is essential – there is little point in having elaborate procedures to deal with complaints if no one knows of their existence or how to use them. Therefore practices have to give the procedure publicity and this can be done in a number of ways including:

- a waiting room poster
- a simple leaflet explaining how the practice deals with complaints
- a section on 'rights and responsibilities' in the practice information leaflet.

Part of the information package needs to make it very clear to whom people should take their complaint. One person needs to be identified by name or job title for that key role, and it obviously makes sense to have a deputy to cover any absence of the usual person. Although some GPs may wish to take on this role themselves, in many practices the practice manager will have the necessary skills to undertake this very sensitive role.

As well as knowing the name of the complaints administrator, people also need to know how to make their complaint. This is the ideal opportunity to emphasize how much better it is to let a practice know as soon as possible about any unhappiness there may be. The sooner a problem is sorted out, the better for everyone concerned. This point needs to be as clearly understood by all members of the practice staff as it is by patients. There is no substitute for common sense, and if someone complains to a receptionist about an unhelpful attitude or an appointment having been written down on the wrong date, then it is obviously better for that to be sorted out straight away by the person concerned rather than diverted into the formal practice-based procedure.

Anyone whose problem cannot be sorted out as immediately as that should be asked to contact the complaints administrator and given a copy of the practice complaints procedure. It is often helpful to give a choice of methods, including:

- an appointment with the complaints administrator
- the opportunity to discuss the problem with the complaints administrator by telephone
- filling in a standard complaints form
- a letter setting out their concerns as simply and as clearly as possible.

All complaints must be:

- recorded in writing
- acknowledged, either orally or in writing, and
- properly investigated.

The timescale for the acknowledgement is within the period of three days beginning with the day on which the complaint was made. Essentially this normally means two working days because Saturday, Sunday, Christmas Day, Good Friday and Bank Holidays are excluded. On occasions it will not be possible to meet that timescale and in those circumstances the acknowledgement should be made as soon as reasonably practicable. The acknowledgement need only confirm that the practice has received the complaint, that it will be looked into as soon as possible and that a further response will be provided as a matter of urgency. It is a good idea for that letter of acknowledgement to include a phrase about being sorry that the problem has arisen. On occasions it will prove possible to provide an explanation as to why the problem arose as part of the acknowledgement. There is no need to separate artificially the process in those particular instances.

Investigating complaints, which have not been immediately dealt with at the time at which they arose or at the time of acknowledging the complaint in writing, should normally be completed within ten working days. This timescale is deliberately short and should lessen the risk of grumbles growing out of all proportion. Thoroughness and fairness should not be sacrificed to speed, and if for example a GP or member of staff central to the complaint is on holiday, the investigation will necessarily take longer. In these cases, it is not only a matter of courtesy but of common sense to keep the complainant informed.

The investigation of an individual complaint clearly needs to be tailored to the circumstances. Although some matters can fairly readily be resolved, for instance where there is an unreasonable expectation on the part of a patient or a simple mistake has been made by a member of staff, the majority of complaints tend to have several contributing factors. The scenario in which a patient telephoning for an urgent appointment gets a hostile reception, followed by a reluctantly given appointment, is then made less than welcome by the receptionist when arriving at the surgery and then has a consultation with a rather harassed GP whose assessment of the patient is perhaps rather prejudiced by the background information given by the practice staff about the 'difficult patient', is not uncommon.

If the patient goes on either not to get better as soon as expected or develops a more worrying medical condition then the combination of those events, none of which in itself might have been particularly significant, can combine to create a very aggrieved individual. In such circumstances the complaints administrator will need to identify all the members of staff concerned, take careful statements from them and be in a position also to involve the GP who actually saw the patient.

Confidentiality is essential to the process of investigation. Where the person complaining is not the patient, written consent from the patient for the complaint to be dealt with on his or her behalf should normally be the rule. Not only the patient but the individual members of staff concerned also need to have their confidentiality protected. There will be occasions on which it is sensible to invite the complainant to meet the member of staff and or GP involved in order to try to resolve matters. It can be helpful to ask for help from the health authority's lay conciliator at such meetings, and, depending on local circumstances, CHCs may also be able to help at this stage.

There are three golden rules to be remembered at such meetings:

1   listen carefully

2   learn lessons

3   do not lecture.

Listen carefully and sympathetically to what the complainant is actually saying. This creates a good impression and will help to defuse someone who is obviously feeling aggrieved. It shows that the complaint is being taken seriously, even though there may not be very much substance to it. Having listened, explain the results of the practice investigation. It is very important at this juncture to avoid jargon and complicated medical terms, keep things simple and avoid getting pedantic. It is very irritating to be told 'you did not ring at ten minutes to ten, it was in fact five to ten'.

Often there will be lessons to be learned, both for the patient and the practice. This can be an ideal opportunity to explain how practice systems work. If the complaint reveals that something needs to be changed within the practice, reassure the patient that the necessary action will be taken and that the problem will be properly discussed at a practice meeting, suitably anonymized to protect patient confidentiality.

Avoid lecturing – patients do not want to be told how lucky they are to have a particular GP in the first instance, how everyone is overworked and underpaid and how unreasonable it is for anyone to dare to complain.

The final key ingredient to seeking local resolution is to provide a sympathetic written summary of the outcome. The written response should take the opportunity to include the following points.

- A suitable expression of sympathy.

- A simple resume of the facts.

- An explanation of practice systems and/or clinical matters.

- A proper apology where one is due.

- A reassurance that any necessary corrective action has been taken.

- The hope that this will have resolved the difficulty and a reminder to the person that if they wish to ask the health authority to look into matters further they should do so within 28 days.

As with all aspects of general practice, careful record keeping is essential. All complaints should be logged, the investigation and outcome should be recorded, and all those records should be kept quite separate from the patient's clinical records. These records of complaints can then be used as a useful basis for practice audits and will provide the raw data for the annual report to the health authority with the numbers of complaints received.

Appendix

In-house complaints procedure – local resolution

Terms of Service requirements

1   All practices must have and operate a practice-based complaints procedure to deal with any complaints made by or on behalf of patients and former patients.

2 The practice-based complaints procedure applies to complaints made to do with any matter reasonably connected with the provision of general medical services and within the responsibility or control of:

(a) any doctor in the practice, whether a partner or employed by the practice

(b) a former partner of the doctor

(c) any member of the practice staff employed by the doctors.

3 Complaints can be made on behalf of a patient or former patient with their consent, or:

(a) where the patient is a child, by the parent, guardian or local authority or voluntary organization under the Provisions of the Children Act, or

(b) where the patient is incapable of making a complaint, by a relative or other adult person who has an interest in his welfare.

4 Where a patient has died the complaint may be made by a relative or other adult person with an interest.

5 Practice-based complaints procedures require that:

(a) the doctor must specify a person either by name or job title to be responsible for receiving and investigating all complaints

(b) all complaints must be:

– recorded in writing

– acknowledged either orally or in writing within the period of three days

– properly investigated.

6 Within the period of ten days of receiving the complaint, the complainant must be given a written summary of the investigation and its conclusions.

7 Where the investigation of the complaint requires access to the medical record, the complaints administrator must inform the patient or person acting on his behalf if the investigation will involve disclosure of information in those records to a person other than the doctor or a partner, a deputy or an employee of the doctor.

8 The doctor must keep a record of all complaints and copies of all

correspondence relating to complaints, but such records must be kept separate from the patient's medical records.

9   A doctor must inform patients about the practice-based complaints procedure which the practice operates and the name or title of the person administering the process.

4   The Conciliation Process

Jane Hanna

The 1996 NHS Guidance on the new complaints procedures identifies conciliation as an essential service provided by health authorities for practices to support early resolution of a complaint.[1] Conciliation is defined as *'a process of facilitating agreement between practitioner and complainant'*. Conciliation is aimed at fostering genuine communication about the complaint in the same way as mediation services have been encouraged in other contexts of relationship breakdown such as family or neighbourhood disputes.

Why practices need a support service

The new reforms promote local resolution as the most effective way of providing a satisfactory response to most complaints. It follows that those at the front line of providing services to the public will bear a heavy responsibility under the new system and will be required to account ultimately to the health service commissioner for the operation of procedures. This responsibility will be for the full range of complaints that is likely to arise in the NHS and will reflect the special nature of the services provided by health professionals and staff working in this area. In addition to the minor gripes that any organization expects to deal with in delivery of services, NHS staff and professionals will have to cope with complaints of a highly sensitive and complex nature that would strain the skills and experience of most organizations for the reasons identified below.

Complaints in the NHS will often involve a challenge to professional decision-making. In addition they may arise in the context of a continuing relationship of treatment and care where a trust has been assumed between professional and patient and sometimes other members of a family. A complaint in this context represents a breakdown in that trust which is painful for all involved because it goes to the heart of the professional/client relationship. A recent study of complaints against GPs suggests that complaints can be understood as a story of what happened told from the different perspectives of the relationship.[2] Both the complainant and the GP interpret the complaint from the viewpoint of their own experience, interests, knowledge and ideas about the handling of illness. Both parties have different information and understandings and conflict is likely. It follows that although leaving the parties entirely to their own devices may be the ideal, this is often unrealistic due to a natural resistance on each side to seeing the other's point of view. This is supported by another research study of GPs which found that three-quarters of GPs interviewed in one health authority considered complaints to be '*not at all justified*'. Although a practice manager or someone else within the practice may be charged with resolving the dispute, internal relations within a practice may make genuine neutrality difficult to achieve and certainly it may be difficult to reassure complainants that this is so. In this situation, involvement by a genuinely neutral third party, trained and experienced in facilitating dialogue, could be a vital support for a practice seeking to reach a satisfactory resolution.

A complaint will require extremely sensitive handling where it follows a serious or tragic event, in particular bereavement. These complaints are most likely where a death has been sudden and relatives have not been offered the opportunity to meet with those responsible for managing care to discuss the events leading up to the death. In this respect a complaint should be interpreted as a means of initiating such a dialogue. Complaints of this nature are likely to be emotionally charged for all concerned. A conciliator experienced in managing the emotional content of such complaints is a valuable asset in such a situation.

It is worth bearing in mind that complaints involving professional judgements where there has been a serious outcome are likely to be as difficult to resolve and as serious as many of the legal claims that end up in court. In these cases a complaint is an alternative non-adversarial way of seeking to resolve a dispute. Recent research on hospital complainants revealed that when a person brought a complaint their needs were often uncrystallized. At this early stage the bringing of a complaint was a desire to establish communications, to be taken seriously and to receive a response. The kinds of response a complainant was seeking would vary, but included a desire for an explanation, an apology or a concern to prevent the same thing happening to others.[3] This did not mean an automatic pseudo-apology but a genuine engagement on the events leading up to the complaint. It follows that although practice-based resolution provides a window of opportunity to resolve difficult disputes early on, it is an opportunity that can easily be lost. All those involved will be looking for a process that can be trusted because it is fair. Some complainants will, for obvious reasons, need some reassurance that a practice will provide a sufficiently neutral environment. Conciliation can introduce an essential independent element and can introduce practical choices such as meetings on a neutral site.

Complaints may also be complex in the context of a public health service where complaints may give rise to mental health issues or where there are cultural or language difficulties. In these cases a trained and experienced conciliator may help in advising on ways of overcoming problems.

The nature of conciliation

Relationship-focused

Conciliation is particularly appropriate where the complaint has been triggered by a breakdown of trust in the professional/patient relationship. The conciliation process allows both parties to retain control of the dispute by focusing on the concerns of those involved and by fostering dialogue. Conciliation is aimed at resolving the grievance not at forcing a reconciliation or continuation of the relationship where this is not wanted.

At a time when quality targets in the NHS are focused on activity rates which are relatively simplistic quality measures, it is important that broad quality issues arising from the context of the individual treatment situation are taken seriously. Conciliation offers an opportunity by those involved in the treatment relationship to review what has occurred with a view to constructive outcomes which aim to meet the interests of both parties in the dispute. The aim of conciliation is, through a managed process of dialogue, to allow both sides to revisit the events leading up to the complaint to allow for a better understanding for all involved. This is not about forcing compromise but about the parties to the complaint moving beyond polarized positions to identify mutual interests in the resolution of the complaint. Conciliation is aimed at encouraging the parties to attack the problem not the other party in the dispute.

Independent and non-judgemental

The role of the conciliator is facilitatory only. It is not about finding fault, but about helping those involved in the complaint to take responsibility for resolving the grievance. Local resolution will need to have an element of independence to inspire public confidence. A study of complaints against GPs found that just over two-thirds of people who had made a complaint preferred not to approach the doctor concerned before going to the health authority. The health authority must act as an 'honest broker' in this situation. Conciliators are a service that can be offered to complainant and practice alike.

A stress-reducing process

The conciliation process provides a 'safe environment' for the expression of the complaint. The skills of the conciliator, the confidentiality of the process and a neutral or agreed meeting place can contribute to a reduction in anxiety about the complaint and generate an atmosphere that will increase the prospects of resolution.

Existing services

A conciliation service has been part of a package of procedures available to complainants and practitioners to assist the resolution of complaints since 1991. The 1996 NHS Guidance identifies conciliation as an essential service for local resolution. There is only one paragraph in the guidance about the service. This provides that:

- conciliation services may prove essential at practice level
- health authorities will need to have lay conciliators available as a service to complainants and practices
- conciliation is entirely a matter for the health authority, i.e. a matter for local not national initiative
- conciliation services, like all other complaints services will be accountable to the health service commissioner.

A conciliator can be requested by the practice, the complainant who may write directly to the health authority, or at the suggestion of the convenor. In this latter case, the complainant has lodged a request for Independent Review and the convenor decides that there has been insufficient investigation under Local Resolution and returns that matter for further action suggesting that the assistance of a conciliator may be helpful.

Beyond the suggestion that conciliation services may be essential there is no national direction on the nature of conciliation services in the NHS.

Key issues to be developed at the local level

The nature and quality of the conciliation services will depend entirely on local initiatives. There are likely to be wide variations in practice. It is to be hoped that some evaluative research will be done to identify good practice from bad. Some major issues that will require resolution at the local level include those identified below. Given the lack of information collated nationally on local initiatives it is only possible to give my own ideas on solutions.

Identifying cases when conciliation is not appropriate

Conciliation is both a voluntary and private process. It follows that it will not be appropriate in cases where:

- either the complainant or the respondent desires a public airing of the complaint or a public precedent to be set or where a complainant has indicated that they want a large award of compensation

- a complainant has expressly indicated that litigation has been instituted. There are a number of important indications that people are to be encouraged to try the complaints process as an alternative to litigation. A 1996 practice direction for medical negligence cases requires each party in a dispute to state whether Alternative Dispute Resolution has been considered and if not why not and if Alternative Dispute Resolution has been rejected why this is so. Further the Legal Aid Board has stated that in respect of small claims under £10 000 (many of these are claims arising out of bereavement) they may expect the litigant to have pursued a complaint through the new complaints procedures before granting legal aid (this advice from the Legal Aid Board is contrary to the spirit of the NHS complaints procedures and investigation of a complaint must stop if either party indicates that legal action is pending). It is important to recognize that complainants may threaten to sue in a moment of anger, distress or sheer frustration. If such a complainant is asked to identify exactly what they want to achieve they may be persuaded that the complaints system is the more appropriate channel for their grievance. This is particularly likely with bereaved relatives who may have more to gain from a full discussion and engagement with those involved than from an adversarial process

- the conciliator has reason to believe that there is a serious issue of public interest at stake

- either party engages in intimidatory behaviour
- one or other of the parties does not wish to cooperate with a conciliation process.

The confidentiality of the process

The intention under the new procedures is that confidentiality is strictly observed by all involved in the conciliation. The requirement of confidentiality is designed to facilitate openness and cooperation in the resolution of the complaint. Under the new procedures conciliators are advised not to report to health authorities the details of cases in which they are involved. It may be helpful where a conciliation has helped to identify the real point of the dispute, that both parties agree to disclose this to the convenor. In the absence of such an agreement the convenor of an independent review panel should not be entitled to confidential information concerning the conciliation.

Although untested in the English courts, litigation in other contexts has upheld the confidentiality of the conciliation process. In family disputes, for example, the courts have accepted that unless the parties can speak freely and without inhibition, and also without worries about weakening their position in contested litigation if that became necessary, the conciliation process would be weakened. The health service commissioner is also likely to have to take a view on how far anything disclosed in conciliation will be available to his investigations.

Equal access to information and support

For conciliation to work it will be necessary that all involved have equal access to clinical information about the complaint.

- Access to all relevant clinical records.
- Access to independent clinical advice. Currently the conciliation service has the support of independent clinical advisors who have been nominated by the Local Medical Committee (LMC). The role of the advisor is to aid the process of conciliation by providing clinical information. It is not to make a judgement on issues of professional negligence. This is a relatively new role for professionals and one which requires thought and development.
- The role of third parties. The process has also had the cooperation of local community health councils (CHCs) who have often acted in

a support role for complainants within the conciliation process, particularly where a complainant needs assistance in clarifying their concerns. Some local practitioner committees have also also provided advice and support to local professionals who have been complained about.

The cost-effectiveness of a conciliation service

The cost-effectiveness of conciliation services in the context of the new complaints procedure has not been measured. Nevertheless, the cost of unresolved complaints could well mean the unnecessary escalation of a dispute. This may mean the growth in the number of requests for Independent Review, the costs and time-consuming nature of which must be borne by the health authority. The cost of establishing and operating a panel is expected to be in the region of £2 000 to £3 000. Alternatively, a complainant may decide that, after all, it is worth making a legal claim. Serious complaints involving serious illness or bereavement, where there is a concern about clinical management, are often potential negligence actions. Currently mediation of claims is being piloted as a way of reducing costs in this area. Nevertheless it is important not to lose sight of the difference between claims and complaints. Mediation of a legal claim will be of a very different nature from conciliation of a complaint. It is likely to involve significantly higher costs and have a very different focus from conciliation of a complaint. Legal representation is necessarily part of mediation of a claim and mediating issues of medical negligence will continue to be the primary aim. Arguably, conciliation of a complaint gives greater control to the parties themselves in constructing the agenda of the dispute. This will depend on the quality of the conciliator and the conciliation process in facilitating the parties in this way.

Of course not all dissatisfied complainants will choose to escalate a complaint, many may simply give up. Although in the short term this may well produce financial savings in the resolution of complaints, in the medium to long term it may be an indicator that the new system for complaints will have failed and that those who experience health care services will not be listened to after all.

The cost of the conciliation service is presently borne by the health authorities and because the services are being developed locally there is enormous variation in practice between authorities. In some areas, conciliators are employees of the health authority whilst in others conciliators are volunteers who may or may not be paid a nominal loss of earnings and expenses.

Practices are not required at present to bear any of the costs of the conciliation service. Usually a conciliator will interview all parties to the complaint individually before arranging any meeting between parties. A conciliator will also discuss the case with an independent clinical advisor and sometimes confidentially with another conciliator who is acting as a co-worker on a complaint. It is certainly likely that the skills, experience and time resources of the conciliator will be saving practice resources.

Quality and accountability

The conciliation service will of course only be as good as the quality of the conciliators appointed in each area and adequate resourcing of the service. The responsibility for this rests with individual health authorities. The Health Service Commissioner has been critical in the past of health authorities that have failed to adequately resource and support lay conciliators.[4] Health authorities will need to evaluate the quality of the service they are offering with the aim of identifying and developing good practice.

References

1 Department of Health (1996) *Complaints: Guidance on implementation of the NHS Complaints Procedure*. Department of Health 12 March 96 (68) para 5.16.
2 Allsop J (1994) Two Sides to Every Story: Complainants and Doctor's Perspectives in Disputes about Medical Care in a General Practice Setting. *Law and Policy*. 16(2):149.
3 Lloyd-Bostock S and Mulcahy L (1994) The Social Psychology of Making and Responding to Hospital Complaints: An Account Model of Complaint Processes. *Law and Policy*. 16(2):123.
4 Report on the Health Service Commissioner for 1992–93 (Select Committee on the Parliamentary Commissioner for Administration, HC 42, Session 1993–94) note 32, paras 28 and 29.

5 Independent Review

David Pickersgill

When a complainant is dissatisfied with the outcome of the local resolution process, be it concerning a complaint arising in general practice or concerning the actions of a trust or health authority, then the complainant is entitled to approach the complaints officer at the health authority (or trust) and request that the complaint be considered by an independent review panel. The request can be made either in writing or orally and it has to be made within 28 calendar days from the completion of the local resolution process. Those using the process, as well as doctors who may be required to respond, should be aware that the complainant's only right is to make the request – they do not have an automatic right to the establishment of an independent review panel to consider their complaint. The decision as to whether a panel will be established rests with the convener (see Figure 5.1). The convener must acknowledge the receipt of any such request within two days of the request being made.

Action by the convener

The convener is a non-executive member of the health authority. He will of course work closely with the complaints officer and will have access to independent medical advice from a doctor nominated by the Local Medical Committee (LMC).

The first action of the convener must be to obtain a statement signed by the complainant setting out their grievances and why they remain dissatisfied with the outcome of the local resolution process. In certain circumstances the complainant may not wish to use the local resolution process and they must similarly set out their reasons for such a decision. The convener has only 20 working days in which to reach a decision as to whether to convene a panel or not. In seeking the written statement from the complainant, the convener has to ensure that the complainant responds promptly and sets out as explicitly as possible the nature of their grievance. It is also the responsibility of the convener to ensure that the doctor being complained against is aware of the details of the grievance. Health authorities have been advised that in sending this information to a

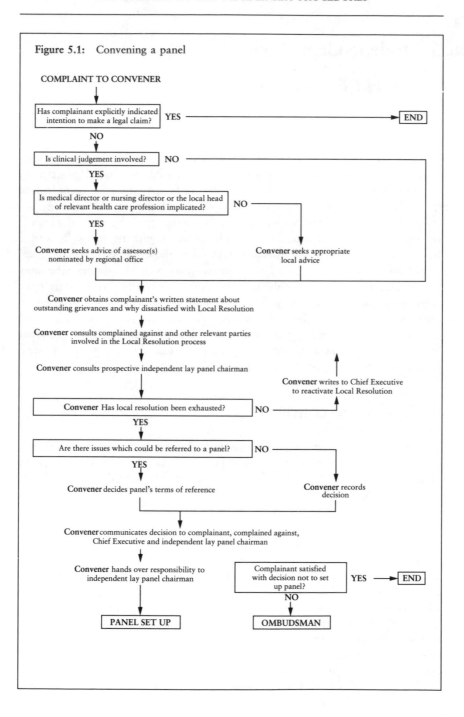

Figure 5.1: Convening a panel

doctor the convener might also like to remind the doctor of the advisability of contacting the Secretary of their Local Medical Committee or other person appointed to assist doctors in responding to complaints.

The guidance to health authorities ('*Complaints – Listening, Acting, Improving*' March 1966 NHS Executive) makes the following important statement in paragraph 6.7: '*When dissatisfied with the outcome of local resolution, a complainant does not have an automatic right to an independent review. There may be occasions when the convener feels that local resolution has been adequately pursued – in that the complaint has been properly investigated and an appropriate explanation given – and that nothing further can be done, although the complainant remains dissatisfied*'.

This puts into practice the expressed wish of the NHSE that the lodging of a complaint should result in an appropriate response and that complainants should not be able to pursue an endless series of investigations merely because they remain dissatisfied with the outcome of an earlier investigation.

Part of the convener's role is to ensure that the complaint is dealt with impartially at the convening stage. It is not their function to defend those complained against, or to appear to be sympathetic to, or take sides with those lodging the complaint. They have to ascertain whether all opportunities for satisfying the complainant during local resolution have been explored and fully exhausted, and what issues if any, could usefully be referred to a panel. Whilst the convener will need to obtain a full picture of the events relating to the complaint, it is not part of his duty to try and resolve the complaint on his own.

To assist them in their task the convener will contact the independent lay panel chairman and in the event that they decide to convene a panel, they will determine the panel's terms of reference. In doing so they will outline the issues which are to be excluded from its consideration, for example matters that have already been dealt with adequately, and detail those matters which will be dealt with. They must advise the complainant in writing of their decision, as well as the Chief Executive of the health authority (HA) and the independent lay chairman of the panel.

In rejecting a request for a panel to be convened it is open to the convener to consider, in consultation with the independent lay chairman, whether the trust/HA/family doctor can take any further action which may satisfy the complainant, or whether they have already taken all practical action and therefore establishing a panel would add no further value to the process. If either of these circumstances applies then the convener should not agree to convene a panel. The NHSE guidance makes it absolutely clear in paragraph 6.12 that a panel should only be convened if the convener considers that it may be able to resolve the complaint and that nothing short of setting up a panel will do so.

In the event that the convener decides to refuse a request for independent review, he must:

- notify the complainant of his decision

- inform the Chief Executive in writing of the reasons for rejecting the request

- inform those who are subject to the complaint of his decision

- inform the independent lay chairman of the prospective panel with whom he has consulted

- inform anyone else with whom he has consulted.

In notifying the complainant of his decision not to convene a panel he must also inform them of their right to refer the matter to the Ombudsman (*see* Chapter 8).

Clinical advice to the convener

The LMC must nominate doctors to act as clinical advisers to the convener. He *must* take their advice in deciding whether to convene a panel when it is considered that a complaint relates wholly or in part to action taken in consequence of the exercise of professional clinical judgement. The exercise of clinical judgement will be involved in various aspects of practice organization as well as in the direct management of a patient's illness. The names of doctors appointed by LMCs will be held by the regional office of the NHSE and will include doctors with relevant experience, including fundholders for complaints which relate to some aspect of the fundholding scheme. Local fundholding groups will assist LMCs in nominating such doctors.

In the event that an independent review panel is established, then the convener will be a member of that panel. If he has decided to refer the complaint back to the local resolution process, or to involve a conciliator on behalf of the health authority, then he may become involved again with a subsequent request for an independent review should the complainant remain dissatisfied with the outcome of such alternative action.

Independent review

Independent review panels will not be anything like the old 'Service Committees'. They will have no disciplinary function. They will not be obliged to conduct formal hearings and they will have complete flexibility to look at each complaint in the way which best suits the individual circumstances. The purpose of the panel is to consider the complaint according to the terms of reference which have been determined by the convener. They will investigate the facts of the case taking into account the views of both sides and then set out their conclusions in a written report. The report will be sent to the person complaining and to the practitioner, and it may contain comments about service improvements. It will not make any recommendations about disciplinary action. That is a matter solely for the health authority to decide after it has considered the report.

The independent review panel will be composed of three members* – the independent lay chairman appointed by the health authority, the convener, and an independent lay person appointed by the health authority. Panel members will be chosen not only for their interest in the subject of complaints, but also for their impartiality and judgemental skills, as well as their proven ability to work in small groups and produce concise reports. In recruiting members to these panels regional officers have to take account of equal opportunities policies and the cultural make up of the communities they serve. None of the people appointed to these panels may be practising or retired NHS staff or members of any of the clinical professions. Although the panels will act as subcommittees of the health authority, no panel member other than the convener should have any past or present link with the health authority which establishes the panel. The guidance issued to health authorities makes it clear that no one lay chairman or panel member becomes regularly linked with a particular trust or health authority (Figure 5.2).

Role of the independent lay panel chairman

The role of the chairman is in two parts: first, to help conveners by providing independent advice and support during the convening period

---

*All of whom will have been nominated by the Secretary of State and whose names are held at the regional office of the NHSE.

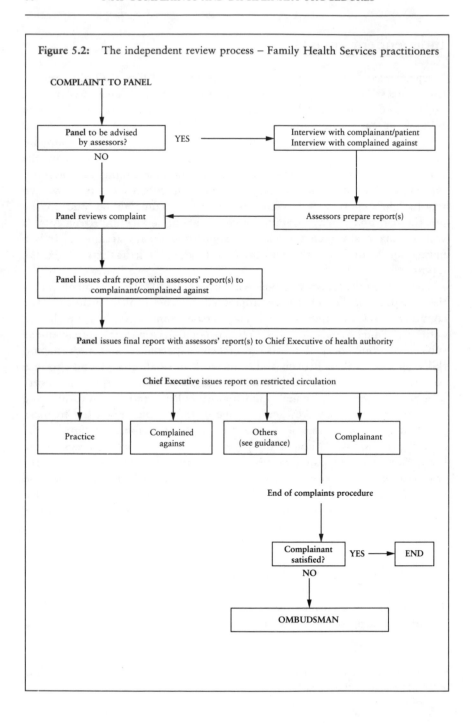

Figure 5.2: The independent review process – Family Health Services practitioners

and second, to lead the work of the independent lay panel. This will involve ensuring a clear understanding of the terms of reference which are provided for the panel. It will be for the chairman to decide on the arrangements for the conduct of the panel's business and to ensure that full records of its activities are kept (these records should be robust enough to withstand any subsequent investigation by the Ombudsman). It is the responsibility of the panel chairman to ensure that the panel and the clinical assessors, if used, have received all the appropriate documentation, including the convener's report, and to agree with the members and the assessors the way in which the assessors will meet with the complainant and the respondent doctor and how they should make their report. The ultimate responsibility for writing the report rests with the chairman and the report should set out the results of the investigations, their conclusions and any appropriate comments or suggestions. The chairman also has a responsibility to ensure that there are no recommendations or suggestions relating to disciplinary matters contained in the report. The chairman may decide with the advice of the panel, to show some or all of a draft report to the complainant and the respondent before the final report is published. Finally, and importantly, it is the responsibility of the chairman to ensure that the panel completes its investigation within the specified time limits and that their report is formally submitted to the Chief Executive of the health authority (Figure 5.3). Throughout the whole process the chairman has the ultimate responsibility of ensuring the confidentiality of the proceedings and of the content of the report.

Clinical assessors

Although the Government's initial intention was for independent panels to be composed entirely of lay members, an important concession about the involvement of clinical assessors was obtained during negotiations between the BMA and the NHSE on implementing the new procedures. There is now written into the procedures provision for either party to a complaint to ask for the involvement of the independent clinical assessors. These assessors will be drawn from a list of names submitted by LMCs and their role is to advise the panel as and when required on those aspects of the complaint which involve clinical judgement.

The assessors will need to consider all the written documentation relevant to each case and will normally be expected to interview both the complainant and the doctor or doctors concerned. They may also wish to interview other witnesses which the complainant wishes to call, or

Figure 5.3:   Summary of time limits/performance targets for independent review process

Event	Time allowed
Original complaint	6 months from event, or 6 months of becoming aware of a cause for complaint but not longer than 12 months from event: discretion to extend
Local Resolution	
Oral complaint	Dealt with on the spot or referred
Acknowledgement	2 working days of receipt, or full reply within 5 working days
Full response by trust/health authority, or family health services practitioner	20 working days of receipt, or 10 working days for practice-based complaints, with extended period if health authority becomes involved
Complainant to apply for Independent Review	28 calendar days of date of response to Local Resolution
Independent Review for family health services practitioner complaints	
Acknowledgement by convener of request for Independent Review	2 working days of receipt
Decision by convener to set up panel, or not	10 working days of receipt of request
Appointment of panel members	10 working days of decision by convener to establish a panel
Draft report of panel	30 working days of formal appointment of panel and assessors
Final report of panel	10 further working days
Final report sent to complainant by Chief Executive of health authority	5 working days of receipt of panel's report

members of the doctor's staff. They will have complete flexibility in how they approach their task, but as previously stated, they should agree with the panel chairman the way in which they propose to perform their duties. The NHSE has set out the following guidance in connection with the role of the assessor (Figure 5.4).

Figure 5.4:   The role of the assessor

The role of the assessors is to advise the panel as and when required, on those aspects of the complaint involving clinical judgements.

The following set of questions is meant to be a framework within which all health care professionals can operate. The questions are meant to be an aide memoire, they will not all be relevant in a particular complaint, so they will need to be tailored to the individual complaint; and they will need to be adapted for each profession.

- Were the actions of the health care professional(s) based on a reasonable and responsible exercise of clinical judgement of a standard which could reasonably be expected of his/her/their peers by patients in similar circumstances?

- Did the health care professional(s) respect the right of the patient (and the relatives/carers with the patient's consent) to influence decisions about his/her care?

- Did the actions of the health care professional(s) conform with the codes of practice and/or rules of his/her/their profession(s)?

- Was the necessary information and/or support and/or expert professional advice available to the health care professional(s) to enable him/her/them to form a proper judgement and offer appropriate care?

- Did the health care professional(s) fail to recognize the limits of his/her/their professional competence?

- If there was delegation to a junior (or subordinate) member of staff of responsibility for the care of the patient, was it agreed and did the health care professional satisfy himself/herself that the junior (or subordinate) member of staff was competent to undertake that care?

- Was there a failure to refer the patient to another health care professional?

NHSE, 1996

The General Medical Services Committee (GMSC) has advised all doctors who are subject to an independent review in connection with a clinical complaint to request the involvement of the independent medical assessors. It should be remembered that the role of the assessors is to advise the panel and the parties to the complaint as and when required on those aspects of the complaint which involve clinical judgement.

Certain other key points should be remembered. Where the complaint is wholly or partly related to clinical matters, at least one assessor will always be present whenever the full panel meets, including meetings with any of those concerned with the complaint. Clinical assessors will, at the panel's discretion, or if requested by either party to the complaint, attend meetings that might be set up between them and individual panel members. Both parties to the complaint will also have an opportunity to speak to the assessors individually. The assessors have the right to ask to interview complainants and when appropriate, to examine them.

Another very important concession obtained during the negotiating process was to secure the guarantee that when the medical assessors have been involved, their comments will be included in the panel's report. If they are overturned or disregarded then the panel's reasons for so doing will be stated. Although it is anticipated that the assessor's comments will normally be produced in a combined report, it is not impossible that they may wish to submit separate reports.

On occasions it may be that a panel chairman feels it would be appropriate to meet the complainant as a way of concluding a clinical complaint and in these instances at least one of the assessors should be present. This is a necessary safeguard to ensure that any clinical findings by the assessors can be fully explained to the complainant.

Finally, it is important to note that in providing the names of assessors for a particular panel the regional office will ensure that the doctors do not come from the same locality as the practitioner involved in the complaint.

The report of the Independent Review

The panel's final report must set out the results of its investigations and outline its conclusions, together with any appropriate comments or suggestions. As previously stated, it must not contain any recommendations or suggestions relating to disciplinary matters. Although the content of the report is confidential, there is a wide distribution list.

The report must be sent to:

- the complainant
- the patient (if a different person from the complainant)
- any person named in the complaint
- any person interviewed by the panel
- the clinical assessors

- the trust/health authority Chairman and Chief Executive

- the doctor complained against.

Additionally, in relation to complaints about the provision of services in hospital or the public health sector, the report must also be sent to:

- the Regional Director of Public Health and Performance Management

- the Chairman and Chief Executive of the independent provider where the complaint is about services provided by the independent sector

- the health authority Chairman and Chief Executive or GP fundholder who purchased the service concerned.

Subsequent action

Once the panel's report is sent to the complainant by the Chief Executive of the health authority the complaints procedure is complete. This must be done within five working days of the Chief Executive receiving the report. It should be accompanied by a covering letter advising the complainant of their right to refer the complaint to the Ombudsman if still dissatisfied. The practitioner concerned should also receive a copy of the report, also accompanied by a suitable covering letter. If the panel has made comment about the possibility or desirability of making changes to a practitioner's services or organization, then the covering letter will contain details of these suggestions. The Chief Executive will tell the complainant that he is inviting the practitioner to respond personally to them on those matters. This same suggestion will be made in the covering letter that goes to the practitioner. The objective is for the entire process to take no longer than three months, from the date on which the request for the panel to be established was made, to the date on which the complainant and the practitioner receive their copies of the report.

It may be that the Chief Executive of a health authority will wish to discuss the findings of a report with the practitioner and he may choose to do this with the assistance of the authority's medical adviser and/or with some input from the Secretary of the LMC. Whilst any suggestions about the provision of services by the practitioner or the organization of his practice will not be binding on the practitioner, doctors would be well advised to consider seriously any such suggestions and to give careful thought to the alternative actions which are open to the Chief Executive of the health authority if the suggestions are disregarded. It is the express wish of Ministers and NHSE officials that on receiving an 'adverse' report, doctors will wish to take remedial action themselves rather than leaving the health authority in a position where it has to consider subsequent disciplinary action. It may be of course that the findings of an independent review reveal matters of such serious concern that the health authority has no option but to invite their Reference Committee (see later) to consider initiating disciplinary action.

Advice to doctors

Doctors should treat all complaints seriously and if a complaint proceeds to the independent review stage, then they should contact their LMC Secretary and/or their medical defence organization without delay. It is not wise to fire off hasty written responses or to try and be obstructive to the smooth conduct of the investigation. Doctors need to remember that the Terms of Service have been amended to include a requirement to co-operate with such investigations. The purpose of the investigation is to ascertain what actually happened on the occasion in question and to provide a full, clear explanation to the patient. It is not about apportioning blame and it is not about finding doctors in breach of their Terms of Service. The new independent review procedure is a much less threatening and less adversarial process than its forerunner, the medical service committee procedure. Whilst it would be unrealistic to expect any doctor to enjoy responding to complaints about the services they have provided, we must try to view them as less threatening than in the past and we must try to adopt a pragmatic approach and acknowledge that from time to time among the thousands of consultations which every doctor undertakes, a few patients will be dissatisfied with the actions of the doctor and that in those circumstances we owe them an explanation. We should also acknowledge that it is patients who use the services we provide and that we may be able to learn from their experience of using those services where deficiencies exist and where we might make changes to improve the provision of the services. We may never share the view of a previous Secretary of State *that complaints are jewels to be treasured*, but we should acknowledge that a helpful and positive approach to the investigation of complaints can only be in our best interests.

6   The New Disciplinary Procedures

David Pickersgill

One of the most significant changes to be introduced under the new arrangements in 1996 was the complete separation of the investigation of complaints from any subsequent disciplinary action. The investigation of complaints is no longer linked to Terms of Service matters. However any subsequent disciplinary investigation must be in connection with matters of concern which raise the possibility of a GP having breached the Terms of Service. The formal system will, as previously, be provided by Regulations under Section 17 of the Health and Medicines Act 1988 and set out in the NHS (Service Committees and Tribunal) Regulations 1992 and subsequently amended in 1996.

Health authorities may become concerned about the possibility of a breach having occurred in a variety of ways, for example, following the receipt of a report from an independent review, directly from the patient's complaint, from routine premises inspections or from financial monitoring. The guidance to health authorities makes it crystal clear that local disciplinary action need not automatically follow when such suspicions are raised – other measures may be likely to produce a more beneficial outcome in relation to the practice of an individual doctor. However doctors need to be aware that in potentially serious cases disciplinary action may be taken at any time, and need not await the outcome of an independent review. In very serious cases the health authority always has the right to make an immediate referral to the NHS Tribunal. The guidance to health authorities states that: *'the yardstick to be used is whether patients are being, and are likely to continue to be endangered by the practitioner's practice or conduct, or whether there are serious financial irregularities'*. If disciplinary action is initiated in such cases, then it will normally halt the investigation of a complaint under the complaints arrangements, but the convenor is given discretion in relation to such a decision.

Main characteristics of the proposals

Flexibility of approach involves:

● emphasis on HAs working with practitioners to uplift standards

- a shift away from explicitly punishment-orientated formal disciplinary arrangements.

A residual service-committee style investigative process to deal with 'difficult' cases which cannot otherwise be dealt with when informal action would be inappropriate.
   These are cases:

- involving alleged serious or repeated breaches of the Terms of Service

- instigated by HAs themselves, rather than a patient. (The proposals are based on the existing system whereby FHSAs can themselves initiate an allegation of breach of the terms of service)

- based on evidence gathered by HAs

- conducted using quasi-judicial procedural rules

- where any penalties considered necessary would be as provided in Section 17 of the Health and Medicines Act 1988, but with greater encouragement of the practitioner to undertake remedial action

- in which there has been a retention of appeal rights for doctors to the Family Health Services Appeal Authority.

It is important to note that the decision to take disciplinary action against an individual doctor can only be made by the health authority with which he is in contract and cannot be delegated to an officer or member of that authority. However the authority may appoint a subcommittee (the Reference Committee) to undertake these functions on its behalf so that decisions can be made speedily between meetings of the main authority. The Regulations require that at least one member of the Reference Committee shall be an executive member of the authority and the guidance reminds them that it would be inappropriate for the convenor to also be a member of the Reference Committee. The minimum number of members is three.
   In considering whether to take disciplinary action the authority or its Reference Committee has a number of options:

- to take no action

- to invite the doctor to take remedial action

- to refer the matter for investigation by a discipline committee

- to refer the matter to an NHS Tribunal
- to refer the matter to a professional body
- to refer the matter to the police.

The guidance to authorities reminds them that disciplinary action is not intended to automatically follow the investigation of a complaint. It is for the authority to decide on the most appropriate course of action bearing in mind the principal aim of securing improvements in services to patients. Authorities are instructed to examine the circumstances surrounding a potential breach of the Terms of Service to identify whether there appears to be a problem which the practitioner could be helped to remedy without the need to refer to a disciplinary investigation. Such circumstances might include, for example, a perceived need for retraining, problems of practice organization or difficulties caused by an exceptionally high workload. They are also reminded that disciplinary proceedings should not be used to punish genuine mistakes, or conscientiously taking decisions which might, with the benefit of hindsight and in the light of events, have been different. It follows that a practitioner who co-operates with locally suggested measures to remedy any deficiencies and one who responds positively to the findings of an independent review, is less likely to find themselves facing subsequent disciplinary proceedings. Clearly stated in the guidance to authorities is the fact that disciplinary proceedings should be regarded as the last resort for use where it is considered inappropriate to try any other action, or where such action has proved unsuccessful.

If the authority or its Reference Committee takes a decision to proceed to a formal disciplinary investigation, then it must identify the specific alleged breach of the Terms of Service. Once this decision has been made it cannot change it subsequently, and it cannot include the addition of new possible breaches during the course of the investigation. Having taken the decision to initiate disciplinary action then the matter is referred to the Chairman of a discipline committee of another health authority. This referral *must* be made within 28 days of the authority receiving the report of an independent review if the disciplinary action is to be taken as a result of a complaint made by a patient, or if the allegation has not been the subject of a complaint, then within 13 weeks of the event concerned. There are no provisions for matters referred outside these time limits to be investigated.

Once the referral has been made the authority has 28 days in which to send the discipline committee its statement of case, which must set out the details of the allegation which it is making and the evidence it intends to introduce in support of the allegation. The statement of case must include the following:

- details of the precise paragraphs of the Terms of Service with which the HA alleges that the practitioner has failed to comply
- for each of the paragraphs details of the alleged failure to comply
- copies of all relevant documentary evidence in support of the alleged failures
- the names and addresses of all witnesses which the HA proposes to call in support of the allegation.

The authority cannot introduce, as part of the evidence it submits, any documents used in the investigation of a patient's complaint. Therefore no statement made by any party to such an investigation can be used automatically as supporting evidence. If the authority wishes to use a complainant's evidence or that of any party to the investigation of a complaint, then it has to obtain fresh statements providing the persons concerned are willing to provide them. It is, however, open to a practitioner as part of their response to an allegation, to introduce statements or documents from the investigation of complaints, but if they do so, then the authority has a similar right to produce as part of its case any documents from the investigation of the complaint which relate to the evidence introduced by the practitioner.

In exceptional circumstances the authority may apply for an extension to the 28-day period for submitting its statement of case, but it must make the application before the end of the initial 28-day period and it will only be granted one further period of 28 days. A practitioner against whom a disciplinary investigation is to take place has 28 days to respond to the authority's statement of case, and similarly may apply for one 28-day extension to this period if they are unable to complete their response within the initial period of time allowed.

The disciplinary hearing

The conduct of the inquiry will follow the old Service Committee pattern. This method of investigation is generally acceptable to the Council on Tribunals and the panel appointed to conduct the investigation will have a lay chairman, three lay and three professional members with a quorum of five. The lay chairman must be a barrister or solicitor. The professional members are appointed by the health authority from a list of nominees provided by the LMC and the lay members will also be appointed by the health authority. For the purposes of appointing disciplinary committees, authorities are encouraged to form consortia in groups of at least three. The advantages of consortium working are that members of disciplinary committees will gain more experience and greater expertise as they will be considering cases on behalf of several authorities rather than only one. It will also make it easier to find sufficient numbers of legally qualified chairmen as only one will be required for each consortium as against one for each health authority discipline committee.

Preparation for a hearing

The health authority which has appointed the discipline committee should give both the 'prosecuting health authority' and the respondent doctor the names of the members of the discipline committee. If any of them are considered by either party to have an interest in the case then they should make their views known to the chairman of the discipline committee who has to consider whether the challenge is reasonable and whether to ask that particular member to stand down and be replaced by a deputy.

The parties will also be asked to give the disciplinary committee the names of any witnesses whom they intend to call and copies of any documents which they intend to present as evidence. They have 14 days in which to submit this information once they have received the letter about the hearing. On receipt of the information the health authority will send it to the other party at least 21 days before the hearing takes place. Both parties will be given written notice of the date of the hearing at least 21 days in advance. Usually the discipline committee will travel to the referring health authority's area to conduct its investigation. Copies of the health authority's statement of case, the practitioner's response and any other correspondence between the health authority and the parties will also be sent to the Secretary of the relevant LMC. Both the authority bringing the case and the practitioner responding will be asked to confirm that they are able to attend the hearing and if not, they must give good reasons for not attending. It is open to the discipline committee to continue with the hearing in their absence if they so wish. If either party ask for a postponement of the date the decision will rest with the Chairman of the discipline committee.

Discipline committees have no powers to invite witnesses or subpoena them, and they have no power to obtain documents for an investigation. It is entirely up to the referring health authority to build its own case and up to the respondent practitioner to build their own defence.

Conduct of the hearing

The Regulations make it clear that disciplinary committee hearings must be held in private and only specified people may attend the hearing. These include the members of the panel, the respective parties and their representatives, and the Secretary of the LMC or some other duly authorized representative of the LMC. As under the old Service Committee arrangements, both the LMC representative and the parties to the hearing must leave when the discipline committee considers the evidence at the end of the hearing. In addition, up to two health authority officers from the Authority which has appointed the discipline committee may attend the hearing to undertake clerical duties.

The respondent practitioner may be accompanied by someone to help them present their case who may either speak to the discipline committee direct, or question the health authority representatives and witnesses. The only exception to this rule is that barristers or solicitors, whether or not they are paid or practising, cannot address the disciplinary committee and cannot conduct questioning or cross-examination of any HA representative or witnesses.

The arrangements at a hearing must be suitable for people who have any disability or special needs and arrangements must be made for interpreters to be present when required.

The first part of a discipline committee hearing is the conduct of the investigation. Both parties and any witnesses will give oral evidence and may be examined and cross-examined by the other party and members of the discipline committee. Once this process is complete then the various parties must leave the room and the discipline committee will undertake its consideration of the evidence it has heard. During the investigatory part of the hearing both parties must be present throughout, and at the outset the Chairman will explain the purpose of the hearing, the procedure to be followed and what will happen after the discipline committee has finished taking evidence. He will also ask if either party wishes to submit any further written or documentary evidence. Such material must be seen by both parties and will only be admitted with the other party's consent, and if the discipline committee agrees it is relevant and admissible.

The proceedings will begin with the health authority presenting its case, following which the practitioner or his representative will have an opportunity to question the health authority, as will members of the discipline committee. The health authority will then call any witnesses which it has to support its case, and again they may be questioned by the authority, the practitioner and members of the discipline committee. Having presented their evidence they will leave unless both the discipline committee and both parties agree that they should remain.

At the conclusion of this stage, the practitioner will then be invited to present his case and confirm his written statement, and the same process of cross-examination will follow. Any witnesses on behalf of the practitioner will then be called and cross-examined and finally, both the health authority and the practitioner will have an opportunity to sum up their cases and add any final comments.

Evidence at discipline hearings is not given on oath and therefore it will be for the discipline committee to decide what credibility to give to the evidence and whether the evidence should be believed if there is a conflict of opinion. Oral evidence which is given by someone who was present at the time of the event and is available to have their evidence tested by questioning is helpful, as is documentary evidence such as letters, certificates and medical records.

If during the course of an investigation a discipline committee finds evidence which suggests the possibility of another different breach, then this must be dealt with as a separate investigation. It can not be investigated at the same hearing.

Clinical judgement

Clinical judgement is now, and always has been, part of a doctor's Terms of Service and discipline committees may have to take it into account when considering whether or not a doctor is in breach of those Terms of Service. It does not necessarily follow that a breach has occurred because a doctor has made a wrong diagnosis, prescribed wrong medication or made an incorrect decision about visiting or the extent of any examination which subsequently turns out to be wrong. A doctor is however required to have reached a reasonable professional judgement in these matters. For example, in making such a decision or judgement has the doctor put himself in a position to reach a reasonable professional judgement? Did he, for example, take an adequate history and make an appropriate examination? Did he use the skill, knowledge and care that all GPs may reasonably be expected to use? If having used that skill, knowledge and care he makes a decision which turns out to be wrong, then he is unlikely to be in breach of his Terms of Service. If conversely he did not use that skill, knowledge and care then a wrong decision could amount to a breach of the Terms of Service. This is not to say that consideration should not be given to the fact that there are genuine differences of opinion within the practice of medicine. The test is whether a responsible body of medical practitioners would think their conduct appropriate. Even though some or all of the professional members of the disciplinary committee may disagree with the doctor's clinical management, his practice may still be acceptable. The medical members of the discipline committee may therefore be asked whether an alternative responsible body of medical opinion would support the action taken by the doctor.

To give a patient all necessary and proper personal medical services a GP does not have to possess the knowledge and skills of a specialist. Paragraph 3 of the Terms of Service requires him to possess a degree of skill and knowledge which GPs as a class possess, and to refer patients to specialists for advice and treatment when necessary.

Standards of proof

The standard of proof used in discipline committee cases is the civil standard, which requires decisions on disputed evidence to be reached on the balance of probability. This standard is flexible and can be higher or lower depending on the nature and seriousness of the allegations. The more serious the allegation to be proved, the more convincing the evidence must be. If both versions of the event have equal weight, then the discipline committee may not prefer one version to the other. It must therefore find one version of the event more probable than the other for the allegation to be proved and it must indicate in its report which version is more probable and why.

The Discipline Committee Report

The information to be contained in the report of a disciplinary committee is set out in paragraph 7 of Schedule 4 of the Service Committee and Tribunal Regulations. It must include:

- a record of the written evidence

- a record of any material oral evidence taken at a hearing before the discipline committee

- consideration of the evidence resolving conflicts of material fact

- a statement of the facts which they believe is relevant on the evidence placed before them

- the inferences which the committee considers may be properly drawn from the facts

- whether the practitioner has been found in breach, or otherwise, for each provision of the Terms of Service identified by the HA in their statement of case and their reasons for reaching that opinion

- their recommendation on the action, if any, which should be taken.

It is also open to the discipline committee to recommend whether a copy of its report should be sent to professional registration bodies such as the GMC. If it does decide to recommend such a referral it should state its reasons for so doing. However, such a recommendation and reasons are not part of its report of the investigation and should be the subject of a separate communication to the health authority.

The report of the discipline committee, together with its recommendations, are sent to the Chief Executive of the authority which initiated the action. The reports will then be considered in the confidential closed part of the meeting. The decision is final unless there is an appeal to the Chief Executive of the FHS Appeal Authority. Only the doctor who is the subject of the investigation can appeal.

The referring health authority is bound to accept the discipline committee's findings of fact and the inferences which they have drawn from those facts as to whether or not the doctor is in breach of his Terms of Service. They therefore cannot amend the discipline committee's conclusions. They do however have discretion when considering recommendations as to penalties. In considering such recommendations they may wish to take into account any previous breaches of Terms of Service by the doctor within the last six years. If they decide not to accept the discipline committee's recommendation then they must state their reasons for so doing in writing. They also have the right to refer the report to the GMC whether or not the discipline committee has made such a recommendation.

A copy of the discipline committee's report and the decision of the health authority will be sent to the practitioner as soon as possible after it has made its decision. It will also notify the practitioner of their right to lodge an appeal and will send a copy of the report to the Appeal Authority.

Only where the health authority feels there is a compelling public interest will it release a summary of the case to the press. If they do decide to take such action then their summary must not include names and other details from which parties could be identified.

Referral to the GMC

The criteria to be used in considering whether a case ought to be referred to the GMC are as follows:

- clear neglect or disregard of professional responsibilities to patients
- an NHS Tribunal decision that a doctor's name should be removed from the Medical List
- irregular certification under National Insurance rules
- irregular charging of fees to patients
- fraud or improper claims for fees
- any canvassing for or gaining patients by unprofessional means.

Penalties

Although the referring health authority is encouraged to recommend remedial action before initiating disciplinary procedures, the options for penalties once a disciplinary investigation has been undertaken are restricted to the following:

- a warning to the doctor to comply more closely with their Terms of Service
- a reduction of the doctor's list size in certain circumstances
- a financial withholding.

In the event that a warning is considered appropriate then it may be accompanied by advice regarding remedial action.

As previously described, another possible outcome is referral to the GMC.

The new disciplinary procedures are intended to be used only when all other options have been exhausted or are considered inappropriate. It follows that they are a serious matter and should be treated as such by any doctor unfortunate enough to be the subject of a disciplinary process. Any such doctor would be well advised to contact the Secretary of their LMC without delay for advice and also their Medical Defence Organization. It is hoped that the introduction of a process for suggesting remedial action will remove the need for many doctors to be referred to a discipline committee and doctors would be well advised to co-operate in any remedial process which is offered.

7 Appeals

David Pickersgill

The new NHS complaints and disciplinary procedures bring significant changes to the appeals mechanism. As the new procedures provide only for the investigation of a complaint, there cannot be any appeal by either party against the result of that investigation. If a complainant is dissatisfied with the outcome of the local resolution process, they may view their right to approach the health authority and request an independent review as a form of appeal. However, this is not the case and as explained earlier in this book (Chapter 5) an independent review can only be convened when there are good grounds for considering that the local resolution investigation has been inadequate or failed to address the matters in question. Although either party to a complaint may not be entirely happy with the report produced as a result of the local resolution inquiry, or at the conclusion of an independent review, there cannot logically be any grounds for appeal. Both processes are designed only to investigate the complaint and to produce a report. They do not take evidence on oath and they do not produce a report which contains 'findings of fact'.

The only part of the procedure where an appeal will be permissible is in relation to the new disciplinary procedure. It follows that if the health authority is acting as the complainant and that the matter is being pursued by its own disciplinary panel, then it cannot appeal against the finding or penalties imposed. Therefore the only party to a disciplinary hearing who now has the right of appeal is the doctor who is the subject of the disciplinary inquiry. There are specific conditions which apply to the lodging of appeals and these are detailed in Regulation 9 of the Service Committee and Tribunal Regulations (the title of these Regulations is now a misnomer as service committees no longer exist) (Figure 7.1).

In practice appeals are made to the FHS Appeal Authority which acts on behalf of the Secretary of State. The address of the Appeal Authority is as follows: The FHS Appeal Authority, 30 Victoria Avenue, Harrogate, HG1 5PH.

A doctor who wishes to appeal must do so within 30 days beginning on the date on which notice of the authority's decision was sent.

When the appeal is against an authority's determination regarding the question of whether or not the doctor is in breach of his Terms of Service,

---

Summary of Regulation 9 paragraph (1)

An appeal may be made to the Secretary of State by a practitioner against the FHSA's determination:

(a) that he has failed to comply with any one or more of his Terms of Service

(b) that action should be taken under Regulation 8 to:

-   impose a special limit on the number of persons from whom the doctor may provide treatment
-   recover expenses from him
-   recover from him an amount not exceeding £500

(c) that there has been an overpayment of his remuneration.

Figure 7.1: NHS (Service Committees and Tribunal) Regulations, Amendment Regulations 1996

or with regard to the question of overpayment of remuneration, the Secretary of State should consider the whole of the complaint or reference on the basis of the evidence available to the disciplinary committee and any further evidence produced on appeal.

The persons appointed to consider the appeal should find facts from which they should draw inferences. If the appeal is against an authority's determination regarding the question of whether or not the practitioner is in breach of his Terms of Service, the Appeal Authority should determine whether or not the practitioner failed to comply with any one or more of the Terms of Service and whether any, and if so, what action should be taken. The authority may determine that a special limit on a doctor's list size should be imposed, and/or that there should be a recovery of expenses from the practitioner, and/or that he should be warned to comply with his Terms of Service. The authority also has the option of taking action with accordance to Regulations 13 and 14, i.e. that there should be a recovery from the practitioner's remuneration.

Where the appeal is against an authority's determination regarding an overpayment, the Appeal Authority determines whether or not there has been an overpayment and, if so, of what amount.

The Appeal Authority may also determine that no further action should be taken.

Procedure

The Regulations also describe the procedure on appeal. If the authority considers that the appeal discloses no reasonable grounds, or that it is otherwise vexatious or frivolous, it may determine that the appeal be dismissed (Regulation 11 paragraph 1). The appellant doctor may, with the consent of the Secretary of State, withdraw the appeal at any time before it is determined if they wish not to pursue their appeal (Regulation 10 paragraph 6).

Unless the Appeal Authority dismisses the appeal as discussed above, a copy of the notice of appeal must be sent to any person who was a party to the proceedings before the disciplinary committee, and to the health authority inviting their observations on the appeal within 30 days of the notice of appeal being sent to them. In appeals relating to overpayments, however, the notice of appeal has only to be sent to the respondent in the appeal, i.e. either the practitioner or the health authority.

It is open to the Appeal Authority, if they consider that an appeal can be properly determined without an oral hearing, to dispense with such a hearing and determine the appeal on the papers. This used to occur under the old appeal system and is only used when there is no dispute as to the findings of fact at the disciplinary hearing or when any new material subsequently submitted in support of the appeal would not materially alter those findings of fact. However, paragraph 5 of Regulation 11 provides the practitioner with a prescriptive right to an oral hearing of the appeal when the appeal is against the health authority's decision to find him in breach of his Terms of Service and they have determined or recommended that there should be a recovery from his remuneration, or in medical cases, that there should be a special limit on the number of patients on the doctor's list.

When there is to be an oral hearing the Appeal Authority will appoint three persons to conduct the hearing. The chairman must be a barrister or a solicitor. The two other persons appointed to hold the inquiry should be members of the same profession as the practitioner concerned. In the case of general practitioners, one of the professional members of the persons appointed will be selected from a panel of names which is provided to the Appeal Authority by the General Medical Services Committee (GMSC). These are doctors in active clinical practice who have experience of hearing complaints and many of whom are members of the Statutes and Regulations Committee of the GMSC. Other members of the panel may be drawn from names submitted by LMCs. These names will usually be doctors with extensive experience of handling complaints at local level and who are considered to be familiar with the Terms of Service for doctors.

The Appeal Authority will give the appellant doctor not less than 21 days written notice of the date, time and place of the hearing and to any other interested parties, which in practical terms means the health authority and any other witnesses that the doctor chooses to call. The appeal hearing is held in private and the only persons admitted will be the parties to the appeal, their representatives, an officer or member of the relevant health authority and the witnesses when they are called.

At the inquiry evidence is given on oath and the parties are usually represented by a barrister or solicitor. Any doctor mounting an appeal should consult his defence organization who will usually, but not always, appoint a barrister to act on behalf of the doctor and present his case. No new material should be introduced unless notice has been given to the Appeal Authority at least seven days before the inquiry, giving details of the facts and contentions which are to be introduced. Exceptionally, new material may be introduced on the day of the inquiry, but only with the consent of the persons appointed to conduct the inquiry.

At the conclusion of the inquiry the 'persons appointed' will submit a report to the Chief Executive of the Appeal Authority and it is the Chief Executive who takes the ultimate decision on the appeal on behalf of the Secretary of State. He will then give written notice to the various parties to the appeal of his determination, together with the reasons for his decision.

The Medical Advisory Committee

When a health authority makes a recommendation that a financial withholding should be imposed, the case will be referred to the Medical Advisory Committee (MAC). This Committee is established under Schedule 5 Part 2 of the NHS Service Committee and Tribunal Regulations 1992. It reports to the Chief Executive of the FHS Appeal Unit and its function is to advise him on any action he should take when a withholding is contemplated. The Chief Executive is required to consult the MAC in the circumstances shown in Figure 7.2.

Where the breach comes under (d) in Figure 7.2 it includes referrals not only to other services provided under the Health Services Acts, but also the provision of advice to enable patients to take advantage of local authority social services. It should be remembered that the Chief Executive of the Appeal Unit may, and frequently does, refer other cases to the MAC as well.

If a practitioner has appealed against an HA's decision, or wishes to appeal against a proposed recovery from his remuneration, the papers sent to the MAC include his written statements or, if there has been a hearing, the report of the persons appointed to hear his case (the report of the appeal).

(a) a failure to exercise reasonable care and skill in the treatment of a patient

(b) a failure to visit, or to treat, a patient whose condition so requires

(c) a failure to order, or to provide, any necessary drug or appliance for the use of a patient

(d) a failure to discharge any obligation on a doctor to give a patient the requisite assistance to enable him to obtain any treatment which is not within the scope of the doctor's obligations under his Terms of Service.

Figure 7.2: Extract from Schedule 5 to Regulation 13 (2)(3) of the NHS (Service Committee and Tribunal) Regulations

The MAC has six members who are appointed by the Secretary of State. The Chairman is a doctor who is required under the provisions of the Regulations to have been engaged in the provision of medical services under the Act for not less than ten years and has been selected after consultation with the GMSC. Usually this doctor will be someone who has been employed by the NHSE as a Regional Medical Officer. Of the remaining five members, three are doctors (GPs) selected from the doctors panel. This panel consists of doctors who have been nominated by the GMSC, and may include non-GMSC members who have been recommended by their LMC for their experience in disciplinary procedures. The GMSC only nominates doctors who are still actively engaged in general practice. The other two doctors on the MAC come from a pool of doctors nominated by the NHSE and they too must have had not less than ten years experience of providing general medical services.

The MAC normally meets monthly and considers the papers from the earlier hearings of the cases before it. It has no powers to challenge the findings of fact and it cannot overturn a decision that a doctor is or is not in breach. Its duty is to consider the withholding which has been recommended and to ensure that similar levels of 'penalties' are applied across the country as a whole. It may recommend to the Chief Executive that no financial withholding is made and that the doctor is merely warned to comply more closely with his Terms of Service. Alternatively, it may change a decision from only a warning to a substantial financial withholding.

Its other function is to advise the Chief Executive on whether or not to refer a case to the General Medical Council (GMC). Under a long-standing arrangement the Chief Executive sends to the GMC cases which have a bearing upon a practitioner's ethical or professional conduct. The Chief Executive does not in any way act as a complainant or make a formal reference to the GMC – he merely passes on information in his possession, normally in the form of the report of the Medical Service Committee and the final decision that he issues on the case. He is not bound to accept the advice of the MAC, but in relation to cases being sent to the GMC he normally does so. The criteria for referral are as follows:

- certain cases involving neglect or disregard of professional responsibilities to patients

- directions by the National Health Service Tribunal that a doctor's name should be removed from the Medical List

- cases of irregular certification under National Insurance rules

- cases of irregular charging of fees to patients

- cases concerning fraud or improper claim to fees

- cases where there may have been canvassing or gaining of patients by unethical means.

Category	No. of cases
Failure to examine	90
Failure to visit	62
Failure to take adequate history	61
Lack of care	43
Failure to refer	42
Inappropriate prescribing	41
Poor administration	23
Breakdown in communication	22
Charging for NHS services	7
Poor record-keeping	7
Poor handling of emergency	7

*Personal communication.

Figure 7.3:   Breaches

Finally, in a recent study* of 188 cases considered by the MAC the breaches found had one or more of the elements shown in Figure 7.3.

A later chapter in this book considers how to avoid complaints and adherence to the advice contained in that chapter would have prevented many of the doctors whose cases were considered in this study, from ever having been found in breach.

8 The Ombudsman

David Pickersgill

'We support the recommendations made by the Select Committee on the Parliamentary Commissioner for Administration to extend the Health Service Ombudsman's jurisdiction to GPs and to the operation by FHSAs of the current Service Committee procedure. We also suggest that the Government should carefully examine whether the practical difficulties might be overcome which the Select Committee believes prevent the Ombudsman considering complaints about clinical judgement.'

Wilson Report, May 1994

In November 1995 the Government published the Health Service Commissioners' (Amendment) Bill. This provided for an extension of the Ombudsman's jurisdiction to include complaints about actions resulting from the exercise of clinical judgement by doctors and other health professionals in providing services in or for the NHS. It also empowered him to investigate complaints about doctors providing NHS family health services, in addition to complaints about NHS hospital and community health services which had always been within his remit. The Bill was enacted on 1 April 1996 with the following main provisions.

- An extension of the Ombudsman's powers to cover complaints about providers of family health services. These services include those provided by GPs, dentists, pharmacists and opticians as part of their undertaking to provide NHS services (Clauses 1 and 2 in the Act).

- To enable the Ombudsman to investigate complaints about actions resulting from the exercise of clinical judgement (Clause 6 of the Act).

- To clarify the Ombudsman's powers to investigate complaints against independent sector providers where they relate to NHS services for patients provided under contract to Health Authorities (HAs), or to Health Boards (HBs) in Scotland, or to NHS Trusts, or to GP fundholders. Independent providers may be private or public bodies, voluntary organizations, or individuals (Clauses 1 and 2 of the Act).

- Clarification that the Ombudsman shall not investigate complaints unless the NHS complaints procedures have been invoked and exhausted by the complainant, save when in his view it was unreasonable to expect those procedures to be invoked or exhausted (Clause 5 of the Act).

- The staff of Health Service bodies (HAs, HBs or Trusts), or FHS practitioners or their staff, may complain to the Ombudsman if they consider that they have suffered hardship or injustice as a result of complaints procedures operated by Health Service bodies (Clause 8 of the Act).

- To enable the Ombudsman where he considers it necessary in the interests of the protection of the health and safety of patients, to disclose information about any person discovered in the course of an investigation to a statutory professional regulatory body, the employing Health Service body, FHS or independent provider, and where the information relates to an FHS provider, to the HA or HB with whom the provider has made undertakings to provide FHS.

Jurisdiction of the Health Service Commissioner

The office of the Health Service Commissioner (Ombudsman) has been in existence since 1973. The statutory powers and responsibilities which he enjoys are set out in the Health Service Commissioner's Act 1993. There are separate offices for Scotland, Wales and England but they have always been occupied by the same person who has also held the office of Parliamentary Commissioner for Administration.

Prior to April 1996 the Ombudsman was able to look into complaints about the NHS where he was satisfied that the complainant had suffered hardship or injustice as a result of maladministration, or a failure in service including non-provision of service when the complaint falls within his jurisdiction.

The Ombudsman must first satisfy himself that the health service body complained of has had a reasonable opportunity to investigate and reply to the complainant. He is not able to look at complaints which are put to him more than one year after the complainant became aware of the matter complained of, unless he considers there are special circumstances which make it reasonable for him to do so. Complaints made to his office are initially screened to see if they come within his jurisdiction. If they do and if the various other requirements are met then he will inform both the complainant and the health service body of the issues that he is going to investigate.

Method of working

The Ombudsman will examine all papers relating to the complaint and also any other papers held by the health service body which he believes to be relevant. He will interview the complainant and those against whom the complaint is made, in addition to any other persons whom he believes may have relevant information to offer.

He produces a draft report which is sent to the health service body before being finalized. This action serves two purposes. First, when he intends to uphold a complaint, it enables the person or body complained against to ensure the factual accuracy of the report. Second, it also enables him to check with that person or health service body what action or actions they propose to take as a result of the report. After any amendments have been agreed the final report is produced and sent to the complainant and the health service body or individual doctor concerned. Selected individual reports and anonymized annual reports are published by the Ombudsman and may form the basis of evidence taken by the Select Committee or the Parliamentary Commissioner for Administration.

The Ombudsman's investigations are conducted in private and he has powers similar to the High Court to require documents and persons to assist his investigations.

The Select Committee

The Parliamentary Select Committee regularly examines his reports and may also examine witnesses from a selection of cases which he has investigated. These witnesses may include individual doctors. Reports of the proceedings of the Committee are published and were an individual doctor to be interviewed by the Select Committee then his identity would become public knowledge. At the time of writing the Ombudsman himself has not decided whether to identify individual doctors or practices in his reports.

Taking a complaint to the Ombudsman

It is important to realize that the introduction of the Ombudsman into the New NHS Complaints Procedures does not mean there is an automatic

right to a third level of inquiry when a complainant remains dissatisfied. As previously stated the Ombudsman will not normally investigate a complaint unless the relevant NHS complaints procedures have been exhausted. This includes both practice-based complaints procedures and independent reviews. In a paper issued in December 1995 by the office of the Health Service Commissioner, the Ombudsman states *'the Ombudsman will ordinarily regard the relevant NHS complaints procedures as exhausted when*:
first:

- *in accordance with the (interim) guidance the complainant has received a response to his complaint from the Chief Executive of the Health Authority of the FHS practitioner and*

- *the complainant has made a written request to the convener of the relevant Health Authority, Health Board or NHS Trust asking for an independent review panel and the convener, after consultation with an independent panel chairman has replied explaining why he will not set up a panel;*

or second:

- *where a complainant has received a report of an independent review panel and, where appropriate, the decision of the relevant NHS body on the findings and any suggestions of the report'.*

The Ombudsman may decide to investigate a complaint where he feels that the responsible health service authority has refused unreasonably to investigate it because it has been received outside the time limit for complaints under the revised NHS complaints procedures. In this context he will need to bear in mind his own statutory time limits. In these cases he will be disposed to look first at whether he should recommend that the NHS time limit should be waived rather than to investigate the substance of the matter to which the original complaint related. He has stated that he is very firmly of the view that it is generally preferable in the first instance for complainants to have their concerns investigated through the local NHS procedures.

Some complainants will no doubt wish to take their complaint to the Ombudsman because they are dissatisfied with the outcome of either the local resolution process or of an independent review panel. In cases where an independent review has been refused by the convener, the Ombudsman will consider whether the convener has given sufficient and adequate reasons for the decision not to convene a panel. If the Ombudsman does not agree with the reasons given he will first generally recommend that a panel be convened, but there may be special circumstances where he feels it inappropriate for a complaint to be investigated in this way and he may choose to investigate it himself.

The Act also gives him discretion to investigate where, in his view, it would be unreasonable to expect the NHS procedures to have been invoked, or as the case may be, exhausted. He may choose to exercise that discretion where there appears to have been excessive delay in the local process, for example in setting up an independent review panel or where local investigations have led to an irretrievable breakdown in a complainant's confidence in the local complaints arrangements.

Criteria effecting the Ombudsman's decision whether to investigate:

- All complaints to be considered by the Ombudsman are subject to a statutory time limit of 12 months from the date on which the complainant became aware that they wished to make a complaint. This may be extended by the Ombudsman if he believes there were special factors which had reasonably delayed the making or pursuing of the complaint.

- If the complainant is not the patient the Ombudsman must ensure that the person making the complaint meets the criteria in the Act to be recognized as a 'suitable person'.

- Where the complaint is against a GP the Ombudsman has to have regard to whether the complaint relates to hardship or injustice caused by the actions, including inactions, of the GP, including employees or others acting on his behalf.

- If the complainant has a right of appeal before a tribunal, or a remedy through the courts the Ombudsman cannot investigate unless he is satisfied that it is unreasonable in the circumstances for the person to resort to that right or remedy.

- He cannot investigate complaints which relate to NHS appointments, removals, discipline or other NHS personnel matters.

- He has to consider whether the matter complained of, and the remedy sought would be better dealt with by investigation by a professional regulatory body such as the General Medical Council (GMC).

- He has to consider whether any other possibilities such as the use of a mediation or conciliation service would be more appropriate than an investigation by himself.

Grounds for investigation

The Ombudsman expects that the majority of complaints will already have been the subject of prior investigations before reaching his office and he will expect the complainant to provide reasons why they remain dissatisfied and still consider that they suffer hardship or injustice. He will need to be convinced in each case that there are sufficient prima facie grounds to warrant an investigation by him, but will aim to ensure that no complaint put to him that should be investigated is rejected, for example, simply because the complainant's initial request does not clearly establish the grounds. A member of his staff may contact the complainant in order to clarify the grounds for the complaint.

Remedies in the courts or at a tribunal

When considering whether to investigate cases where there may be a remedy in the courts or a right to go to a tribunal the Ombudsman will try to clarify what it is that the complainant is seeking. If the primary concern seems to be to obtain damages then the Ombudsman will be disposed not to investigate. He will be similarly disposed where there is evidence that the complainant is already seeking or considering a legal remedy in the courts. He may specifically ask complainants whether they intend to seek or have considered seeking a remedy in the courts although he recognizes that complainants are not legally bound by any assurances they may give in this respect.

In general the Ombudsman will not wish to investigate matters which are being considered by professional regulatory bodies such as the GMC.

Professional advice

The Act confers on the Ombudsman powers to obtain advice from any person who, in his opinion, is qualified to give it to assist him in any investigation, and to pay any such person *such fees or allowances as he may determine, with the approval of the Treasury*. To assist him in this respect he has created the part-time post of General Practice Adviser. This post has been filled by an experienced GP who still works part-time in general practice in addition to her duties assisting the Ombudsman. Additionally his office is able to call upon the services and experience of those doctors who serve on the Appeals Panels and the Medical Advisory Committee for England and Wales to express opinions about the subject of complaints which he may be considering investigating. Thus medical advice will be available to him both at the screening stage and at the detailed consideration and investigation stage.

'Where the statement of complaint includes issues related to the exercise of clinical judgement the Ombudsman will expect his professional advisers to draw on their knowledge, experience and expertise. He will be asking them, as a general rule, to advise him on whether the actions complained of were based on a reasonable and responsible exercise of clinical judgement of a standard which the patient could be reasonably entitled to expect in the circumstances in question. Advisers will be able to take appropriate account of their assessment of the skills, knowledge and experience of the professional concerned and all the other particular circumstances of the case which they consider to have a bearing on the decisions and actions in question. Advisers would not be invited to say whether they personally would have decided or acted similarly or to give advice on whether the action taken is the best possible. The Ombudsman will however expect his advisers, in deciding what was reasonable and responsible in the circumstances, to have due regard to all the relevant professional guidance on standards and good practice which, in their view, a professional working in the capacity in question could be expected to take into account. Where appropriate he would expect his advisers also to consider whether, in the matters complained of, acceptable standards of delegation, accountability, supervision and support had been demonstrated.'

Health Service Commissioner 1996

The Ombudsman has made it clear that whilst he does not wish to encourage or seek to promote a 'blame culture' it is his responsibility to criticize where in his view the patient does not receive the service he is reasonably entitled to expect. It is not his responsibility to set standards. However his advisers, where they see fit, may draw to his attention any aspect of the services provided where they consider improvements could with benefit be made, or action taken to prevent any recurrence of a shortcoming. The Ombudsman may then reflect such views in his report.

Ombudsman's reports

The Ombudsman will be solely responsible for the final report of any investigation undertaken by his office including those which involve issues of clinical judgement. The report will reflect and respond to the particular complaint. He may or may not chose to append to his report the advice he has received from his professional advisers.

His reports have absolute privilege for the purposes of the law of defamation. Neither he nor his staff can be required to give evidence in any court proceedings about matters which come to his knowledge through his investigations. Similarly the advice provided by his advisers will enjoy qualified privilege.

Further information

The Ombudsman has issued an information leaflet for the general public explaining the changes in his powers and his wider jurisdiction. These leaflets are widely available through health authorities and trusts. In addition he has also produced an information leaflet for FHS providers which includes GPs and further more detailed information may be obtained from the Director, Office of the Health Service Commissioner, Millbank Tower, Millbank, London, SW1P 4QP.

9   The NHS Tribunal

David Pickersgill

NHS Executive circular (HSG(95)62) stated that: '*the NHS Tribunal's aim is to protect NHS services by ensuring that they are not brought into disrepute by the continued practice of those who prejudice its efficiency.*' In the case of general practitioners its remit is to decide whether the continued inclusion of a doctor's name on a health authority's medical list would be prejudicial to the efficiency of the service. If it does so decide, then it must direct that the doctor is disqualified from providing the service and that his name should be removed from the authority's medical list. It has no lesser sanction available to it, but it may additionally direct that the doctor's name be removed from or not included in any similar lists of other health authorities and they may also, if they think fit, declare that the doctor is not fit to be engaged in any capacity in the provision of general medical services.

Most, but not all cases considered are based on persistent breaches by practitioners of their Terms of Service with the NHS. Its powers make it the ultimate NHS disciplinary body for FHS practitioners with authority to deal severely with the very worst practice.

Constitution of Tribunal

The constitution of the Tribunal is laid down in Schedule 9 to the 1977 NHS Act. It provides for the appointment of a Chairman by the Lord Chancellor, together with any number of Deputy Chairmen, again appointed by the Lord Chancellor. The Chairman or Deputy Chairman must have a ten-year general qualification within the meaning of Section 71 of the Courts and Legal Services Act 1990 (this means, shall be a practising solicitor or advocate of not less than ten years' standing). In addition, the Secretary of State appoints a number of lay persons and a number of medical practitioners, made after consultation with such organizations as the Secretary of State may recognize as representative of the profession. In practical terms this means doctors who have been nominated by the General Medical Services Committee (GMSC) of the BMA. The functions of the Tribunal shall be exercised by three members consisting of the Chairman or a Deputy Chairman, a lay person and a doctor from the panel of medical members of the Tribunal.

Interim suspension

One of the important amendments introduced in the NHS (General Medical Services) Amendment Regulations 1995 was to provide for the interim suspension of practitioners once an authority had decided to refer the practitioner to the Tribunal. Given that the basis of the authority's case is that the continued inclusion of the doctor's name in the list is likely to be a source of danger to the public, it is perhaps not surprising that this provision was introduced. The authority has to make application to the Tribunal for a suspension order to be made, and there are provisions for payments to be made to the doctor concerned pending the outcome of the Tribunal decision and if necessary, for an extension of those arrangements, and indeed for an extension of the suspension should the doctor choose to appeal against an adverse decision of the Tribunal. Similar provisions exist under Scottish legislation where the relevant Act is the NHS (Scotland) Act 1978.

Procedure

The Tribunal Chairman is appointed by the Lord Chancellor. The members are appointed by the Secretary of State for Health. Usually hearings take place before the Chairman (or his deputy), one lay member and one professional member. The procedure is not laid down in Regulations, but is determined by the Chairman. The parties can be and usually are represented at the hearings by barristers instructed by solicitors. The Tribunal can summon witnesses to give evidence. Evidence is given under oath or by affirmation. The Tribunal will determine the case on the balance of probabilities. It may make awards as to costs.

Suspension

The practitioner has the right to be heard by the Tribunal and to call witnesses and produce evidence before the Tribunal decides whether or not to make a suspension order. In order that suspension applications can be heard as quickly as possible, the Chairman or his Deputy is able to consider suspension applications sitting alone as 'a Judge in Chambers'. Alternatively, he may decide to hear suspension applications before a full Tribunal.

If the Tribunal considers that the practitioner should be suspended in order to protect patients, it may make an order that the practitioner is to be regarded temporarily as being removed from any relevant list. For this purpose the practitioner is deemed to be unfit to provide relevant services in any capacity. This direction is mandatory on the Tribunal at this point, since the question at issue will always be patient safety.

The initial period of suspension lapses when the Tribunal, following a full hearing, disposes of the case by issuing a decision whether or not the practitioner should be disqualified, unless it includes in that decision a further direction that the suspension should continue. The further period of suspension prevents the practitioner returning to practice until his appeal rights have been exhausted or, if he decides not to appeal, until the disqualification direction is enforced by the health authority at the end of the period for appealing.

Disqualification

If the Tribunal makes a decision that a practitioner is disqualified, it may direct disqualification from one HA list or from all HA lists. If it directs that a practitioner's name should be removed only from one HA's list, the practitioner can still work as a principal on the list of some other HA. Therefore at this point the Tribunal has a discretion whether to declare that the disqualified practitioner should not be employed in any capacity connected with the provision of general medical services. The same arrangements are in place for the other contractor professions.

There are parallel arrangements in Scotland and Northern Ireland and if a practitioner is disqualified or suspended by a Tribunal in one of those countries the disqualification or suspension applies in England and Wales as well. Similarly, disqualification or suspension imposed in England applies also in Scotland and Northern Ireland.

Appeals

A doctor against whom a Tribunal has made a decision to remove his name from the list may appeal to the High Court on points of law, and the details of this right of appeal to the High Court are provided by the Tribunal's and Inquiries Act 1992. A doctor who has been so suspended can not be prevented from acting as a deputizing doctor or locum, but there are separate regulations which are intended to prevent principals knowingly employing a person who is subject to such a declaration.

Obviously Tribunal directions can only apply to practice principals as they are the only doctors in contract with HAs for the provision of general medical services.

An application for a suspension order may only be made if the authority has already made representations to the Tribunal that the practitioner should be disqualified. The suspension, if granted, will come into force before there have been any adverse findings against the practitioner and the test for suspension is therefore narrow – the Tribunal must satisfy itself that suspension is necessary to protect patients. Suspension should not be viewed as an additional sanction. It is intended only to protect patients. Suspension cannot be invoked in any other circumstances.

The provisions for protection of practitioners' income during periods of interim suspension are made in the NHS (General Medical Services) Amendment (2) Regulations 1995 and in the Statement of Fees and Allowances.

Removal of disqualification

A doctor whose name has been removed from the medical list by direction of a Tribunal may apply to have the disqualification for inclusion in any list to be removed by the Tribunal. The Regulations provide for further inquiries to be held and for the doctor to appear either in person or to be represented by Counsel or solicitor, or other representative before the Tribunal. On that occasion he may call such witnesses and produce such evidence as he believes will be helpful to his case. He may also request that the hearing be held in public.

It goes without saying that reference of a doctor to the NHS Tribunal is an extremely serious matter which may result in the loss of his livelihood. It is therefore vitally important that any doctor unfortunate enough to find himself in this circumstance should consult his medical defence organization without delay. It should also be self-evident that he would be well advised to be represented at any Tribunal hearing by a solicitor or barrister, that he should co-operate fully with the inquiry and that he should disclose all relevant facts to those people who he chooses to assist and represent him.

Fortunately the number of cases referred to Tribunals has been very small and it may be that with the introduction of the GMC's new performance review procedures there will continue to be only a few cases going to the NHS Tribunal. Nevertheless, its existence and powers should be known to all doctors in NHS practice and the recent introduction of the powers to provide for interim suspension of practitioners indicate that the NHSE sees a continuing role for the NHS Tribunal.

Summary

- The Tribunal is a non-departmental public body with judicial powers supervised by the Council on Tribunals.

- Its purpose is to protect NHS FHS by ensuring they are not brought into disrepute by the continued practice of people who prejudice its efficiency.

- If it decides that a practitioner should be removed from a HA's list it may also decide to exclude him/her from all HA lists.

- It may also declare that the disqualified practitioner should not be employed in any capacity connected with the provision of GMS.

- It also has powers to suspend a practitioner pending a hearing and decision on whether he/she should be disqualified if it considers that this is necessary to protect patients.

- Its powers make it the ultimate NHS disciplinary body for FHS practitioners with authority to deal severely with the very worst practice.

- The right of appeal against NHS Tribunal decisions lies to the High Court on points of law.

10 The General Medical Council

Anthony Townsend

What is the GMC for?

Most people have heard of the General Medical Council (GMC). Members of the public may recall reports in the press of doctors struck off the register for lurid sexual offences; and most doctors, in addition to paying an annual fee for the privilege of registration, will have the GMC's address lurking in the back of their minds, as the feared destination for those members of the profession who find themselves called to account for their actions.

Beyond that, most people, including many doctors, have only a sketchy idea of what the GMC is for, and how it does it. In particular there is often considerable confusion between the functions of the GMC, and the disciplinary and employment functions of NHS employers.

This chapter aims to help doctors, NHS officers, patients and others by explaining:

- the functions of the GMC
- its procedures
- what kinds of cases the GMC can deal with.

The GMC's functions

The GMC's functions flow from a simple purpose: to protect patients, and to guide doctors. To do this the GMC publishes the names of those entitled to practise as registered medical practitioners in the UK.

The register provides the public with the names of doctors who have acquired the necessary medical qualifications and experience to equip them for practice in the UK. For that reason, part of the GMC's function is to set the framework for medical education in the UK, and to ensure that medical students are educated to the standards which the GMC expects.

The other side of the GMC's role is to ensure that, where a doctor has fallen significantly short of the required standards, systems exist to review the doctor's fitness to remain on the register and, where necessary in the interests of patients, to restrict, suspend or erase the doctor's registration. Those systems are called the fitness to practise procedures.

Fitness to practise procedures

There are three distinct procedures which the GMC can use to investigate a doctor's fitness to remain on the register. These are:

1   the conduct procedures

2   the health procedures

3   the performance procedures.

Anyone can complain to the GMC, whether or not other complaints procedures are in train. There is no time limit on complaints, although very old complaints may be impossible to pursue. Members of the GMC (medical and lay) consider complaints, direct further inquiries if necessary, and, where they consider it justified, refer the complaints to a committee which makes decisions on doctors' registration.

Conduct procedures

The conduct procedures are designed to deal with doctors whose actions or behaviour amount to 'serious professional misconduct'. A number of legal definitions of serious professional misconduct exist, but they are not particularly helpful to the ordinary person. A practical guide is that serious professional misconduct is misconduct which is sufficiently serious to call into question the doctor's continued registration. So, for example, a complaint that a patient had been kept waiting for 20 minutes in the surgery waiting room would not merit consideration but a complaint that a doctor had failed to visit a seriously ill patient, despite being given evidence that such a visit was required, would certainly merit consideration.

The conduct procedures can be used for a wide variety of complaints: complaints about gross clinical failings, breaches of confidentiality, dishonest behaviour, improper relationships, and other actions which place patients at risk. Doctors convicted of criminal offences are also dealt with under the conduct procedures.

Complaints are initially screened by GMC members: cases where there is prima facie evidence of serious professional misconduct are then assessed, on paper, by the Preliminary Proceedings Committee, which decides whether a formal hearing is necessary. If a formal hearing is required – and there are around 100 such hearings per year – the doctor appears before the Council's Professional Conduct Committee, in public, and the case is considered in much the same way as a criminal offence is tried by a court.

Doctors found guilty of serious professional misconduct, or of a criminal offence, may face a sanction ranging from an admonition, through conditions which may limit a doctor's practice, to suspension of registration or, where justified, the erasure of the doctor's name from the register. Where a doctor has been erased from the register, they may apply to be restored, but the onus is upon the doctor to show that it is appropriate and safe for them to be returned to practice.

Health procedures

The GMC's health procedures handle the cases of doctors who are suffering from illnesses – almost invariably addiction to alcohol and/or drugs and/or a mental condition – which impair their ability to practise safely.

The procedures are directed by medical members of the Council who, if they are satisfied that there is sufficient evidence that the doctor may have an impairing illness, arrange for medical examinations to take place.

The primary purpose of the procedures is to protect patients. For that reason, where medical examinations show that the doctor has an illness which might impair their ability to practise safety, action is taken to limit the doctor's practice, or if necessary to remove the doctor from practice. Doctors who prove unwilling or unable to co-operate with the GMC's recommendations are referred to a private hearing of the GMC's Health Committee, which has the legal powers to place conditions upon, or to suspend, registration.

In addition to protecting the public, the health procedures also offer expert medical supervision and support to doctors who are prepared to face up to their illnesses, and accept treatment. Doctors who come to terms with their illnesses, and make good recoveries, are returned to full practice, and released from the GMC's supervision, when it is safe to do so.

Performance procedures

From late 1997, the GMC will have a third set of procedures. Unlike the conduct procedures, which consider specific incidents of serious professional misconduct, the new performance procedures are designed to deal with doctors who demonstrate a pattern of seriously deficient performance. Doctors referred to these procedures will have their professional performance assessed by teams of medical and lay assessors and, if necessary, will be asked to accept further training or counselling to remedy their deficiencies. Doctors whose standard of performance presents a serious risk to the public or who are unwilling or unable to be retrained in this way, will face a private hearing, and the possibility of their registration being restricted or suspended.

The interface between the new NHS complaints and disciplinary procedures and the GMC's procedures

It is important to understand that, while cases may be referred from the NHS procedures to the GMC, or vice versa, the GMC's procedures are completely independent.

The GMC's primary duty is to protect patients by investigating cases which call into question a doctor's fitness to remain on the register. For that reason, where necessary, the GMC will act even where NHS proceedings are contemplated or in train. It is a common misconception that cases must go through the full NHS procedures before the GMC can take action. Although there are cases in which the GMC does await the outcome of NHS procedures before acting itself – because there is no immediate public risk, because the NHS procedures may provide valuable evidence to help the GMC assess the case, or for other legal reasons – the GMC alone has the power to remove doctors from all forms of practice for which registration is required, in the public and the private sector. In contrast, the outcome of the NHS procedures may terminate a doctor's NHS employment in one area, but may not prevent the doctor from repeating potentially dangerous actions in the private sector or elsewhere in the NHS.

When in doubt, ask

NHS authorities, medical colleagues and patients are often in doubt about whether it is necessary or appropriate to involve the GMC in a complaint. The GMC is always ready to advise on this kind of question. Where GMC action would not be appropriate, the GMC may be able to suggest other approaches. For the sake of public safety, it is better to approach the GMC when in doubt, rather than allow concerns about a doctor to go unreported for some while. The GMC's procedures, being legally based, and in the interests of fairness to doctors, inevitably take some time from inception to the point at which a doctor's registration may be affected. Early action is, therefore, always to be preferred.

Further information

Further information about the GMC generally may be obtained from the GMC's external relations office (telephone: 0171 915 3509; fax: 0171 915 3641; address: 178–202 Great Portland Street, London W1N 6JE).

11 The Role of the Local Medical Committee

Tony Stanton

The NHS Act makes provision for health authorities to recognize Local Medical Committees (LMCs) as being representative of general practitioners in their respective area. Each LMC has a constitution usually modelled on one previously agreed between the Secretary of State and the GMSC, and which meets the requirements of the GPs in the area concerned and has been approved by the health authority.

The vast majority of LMCs have a medically qualified Secretary – a minority have lay people fulfilling that role, but with other qualifications, for example legal or management expertise. Most of the post holders are employed on a part-time basis, but there is an increasing trend towards full-time Secretaries who in turn often serve more than one individual LMC.

As with many aspects of the work of LMCs, their involvement in the complaints procedures includes a number of facets:

- statutory
- informal custom and practice
- nomination of doctors to assist with the complaints procedures
- advice to doctors receiving complaints
- assistance to and representation of GPs at complaints investigations and disciplinary hearings
- pastoral support.

Some GPs are understandably, if unnecessarily, concerned about issues of confidentiality in relation to the involvement of LMCs with complaints investigations and disciplinary procedures. In reality, it is the LMC Secretary who is normally responsible for ensuring the provision of help to individual GPs. Although LMCs make the nomination of doctors to assist in the investigation of complaints and discipline procedures, their discretion and confidentiality can be relied upon.

Misunderstandings can also arise as to the division of responsibility between LMCs and Medical Defence Organizations (MDOs) in the field of complaints. Clearly it must be for the individual doctor to decide whom to approach for assistance. Continuity and consistency of advice are very important when dealing with any complaint. There is normally very effective liaison between LMC Secretaries and the major MDOs which can prove most fruitful, subject of course to the consent of the practitioner.

Many LMCs arrange with their health authority for an offer of help to be made to doctors when the authority first contacts a doctor in relation to a complaint. Help is usually offered in one of three ways:

1   By the health authority simply giving the name address and telephone number of the LMC Secretary.

2   By the health authority including a pre-printed letter from the LMC Secretary offering help.

3   By an arrangement whereby the health authority informs the LMC Secretary that a complaint is being forwarded to a particular doctor leaving the LMC Secretary to make contact direct.

The pre-printed letter, although it can seem rather impersonal, does have the advantage that there is no risk of the perception of confidential information having been divulged and it does provide an opportunity to set out a series of do's and don'ts which many GPs find very helpful.

Such a letter is a useful way of the LMC reminding doctors that it is indeed a Terms of Service requirement to have in place practice-based systems for handling complaints, and to co-operate with health authority complaints procedures.

Learning of a complaint via the health authority can come as a shock to the system, irrespective of whether the practice has already tried to deal with it in-house or the complaint has gone direct to the authority.

Any GP receiving a letter to do with a complaint from the health authority needs to read it very carefully, and to check carefully as to what it is they are being asked to do. There are five key questions for the GP to consider.

1   Are you being reminded to use the practice-based procedure?

2   Are you being asked to have a second attempt at resolving the matter at practice level?

3   Are you being asked for a reasoned and sympathetic written response to the complaint?

4 Are you being asked to take part in conciliation?

5 Is the health authority starting an independent review?

Having read the letter, there are then several key don'ts.

- Don't panic.

- Don't ignore the health authority's letter.

- Don't feel ashamed – you are not alone in receiving a complaint.

- Don't rush into replying.

- Don't delay the response beyond the time limit – if you need more time, ask.

At the same time, the letter from the LMC can remind the doctor that if the health authority is proceeding to an Independent Review, any clinical matters will require the appointment of two independent clinical assessors, GPs nominated by LMCs and based outside the GP's health authority area. It is also an opportunity to emphasize that Independent Review panels are not like old Service Committees and they have no disciplinary function. They are meant to look at complaints flexibly and constructively. If there is a clinical component to the complaint, the doctor can be reminded to ask for the appointment of clinical assessors.

Following on from the list of don'ts, there is an equally important list of do's to remember when dealing with any complaint.

- Collect together all relevant records including the patient's clinical record, visits log, telephone message log, appointment sheet etc.

- If the complaint reminds you of something relevant which is not recorded in any of those records, make a separate record and keep it as an aide memoire for later use.

- **Do not under any circumstances alter any records, even for the sake of clarification.**

- Ask practice staff who have been involved in the circumstances of any complaint to provide a simple statement of their memory of events.

- Remember that complaints concerning community staff working with your practice should be dealt with by the community trust concerned.

- Return patients medical records to the health authority as soon as possible if you are asked to do so.

- Take copies of those medical records before you return them.

- Keep the records of an investigation of a complaint quite separate from the patient's medical records.

Since doctors are universally expected to be saints, the LMC letter can remind doctors that however irritating, trivial or vexatious the complaint may appear to be, there are some simple golden rules in formulating the response.

- Try to be sympathetic.

- Avoid jargon and use plain English.

- Don't be afraid to say sorry – an apology is not an admission of negligence.

- Protect the confidentiality of the patient and of the practice staff.

- Don't request the removal of the patient from your list simply because they have made a complaint.

- Ask for advice, and ask for it early.

Despite any help GPs may have had in carrying through their practice-based investigation, rounded off with a letter summarizing the action taken and the outcome, there will inevitably be complainants who will wish to take further action. The time limits require complainants to apply to the health authority for Independent Review within 28 days of that summary letter. Those requests have to be screened by the health authority's convener, who has a number of options.

- Inviting the practice to reconsider the complaint.

- Exploring whether conciliation may help.

- Consulting with a nominated independent lay panel Chairman before proceeding with an Independent Review panel.

- Deciding not to take further action.

Any general practitioner notified by the health authority of any course of action proposed by the authority's convener would normally be very well advised to take advice before agreeing to any informal course of action or before responding to a panel investigation. The LMC Secretary should be a prime source of contact in that situation.

If a panel is convened, the person who chairs that panel has considerable flexibility to decide the exact mechanism by which the panel will do its work. There are, however, two golden rules to remember:

1 Where the complaint is wholly or partly related to clinical matters, panels must be advised by at least two independent clinical assessors on relevant matters.

2 When being interviewed by any members of the panel or the clinical assessors the GP may be accompanied by a person of their choosing, who may, with the agreement of the panel Chairman, speak to the panel members/assessors (a legally qualified person acting as an advocate is excluded). There is considerable merit in GPs always seeking to have someone with them at such interviews, and especially bearing in mind the importance of local circumstances to have someone nominated by the LMC will often be beneficial.

The panel's first report has to set out the results of its investigations, outlining its conclusions, with any appropriate comments or suggestions. The panel is not a disciplinary body nor can it make recommendations relating to disciplinary matters.

Both the complainant and the general practitioner will be provided with a copy of the report, and it is open to GPs to discuss the report in confidence with their LMC Secretary if they wish. The advantages of sharing that report include:

• the opportunity to discuss how to respond to any suggestions the report makes

• pastoral support and stress counselling

• a chance for any GP to consider complaining to the Ombudsman if they consider that they have suffered hardship or injustice through the complaints procedure operated by the health authority.

Many LMCs are also working with health authorities to set up mechanisms by which a joint approach might well be made to GPs as a follow up to independent reviews. This rather more interventionist role for LMCs should not be seen as a threat but as an opportunity to colleagues to be in a position to help in circumstances where a health authority is looking to remedy a problem without a disciplinary investigation. Examples of such situations might be where there have been suggestions of:

- a need for re-training

- practice organization problems

- difficulties caused by an exceptionally high workload.

In the circumstances where a health authority chooses to take a potentially serious matter further, it has a number of choices including:

- a discipline committee of another health authority; and/or

- the NHS Tribunal; and/or

- the GMC; and/or

- the police.

General practitioners faced with an investigation by any of these four bodies would obviously be well advised immediately to consult their Defence Organization. In terms of Discipline Committee investigations, which will be solely concerned with an allegation that a practitioner may have breached the Terms of Service, LMC Secretaries will normally have the expertise to be able to guide their constituents through the complexities of the process and to assist them at a hearing. The essential rule for a GP asked to respond to a Discipline Committee investigation is not to put anything in writing without first having taken advice. It is also very unwise to go to a Discipline Committee hearing unaccompanied. The rules permit another person to assist the GP in the presentation of their case, and that representative must be allowed to be present throughout. If the person accompanying the doctor is a barrister or solicitor, then that person will not be permitted to address the committee or question any witnesses. Whether or not the GP has asked for help from the LMC, the Regulations do permit a member or officer of the GP's LMC to attend as an observer.

Any GP found in breach of the Terms of Service does have the right of appeal. Appeals can only be made by practitioners. They may appeal against the health authority's:

- finding of fact or inferences

- determinations about warnings, financial penalties, or impositions of special limits on list size

- determinations about overpayments.

Notice of appeal has to be given in writing within 30 days, and LMC Secretaries would normally be able to liaise with the doctor's defence body in formulating a concise statement of the grounds of appeal.

Finally, complaints are sometimes made by one doctor against another, and an LMC does have power under the Regulations to consider any complaint made to it by any doctor against a doctor providing general medical services in that locality which involves any question of the efficiency of such services. This should not be seen as an invitation to 'shop a Doc', but as one way in which perhaps potentially more serious difficulties may be avoided in the future.

12 The Role of the Medical Defence Organization

Peter Schütte

Introduction

The Medical Defence Organizations (MDOs), together with the British Medical Association (BMA), provide a comprehensive service to advise and assist their members at all stages of the NHS complaints and disciplinary procedures and with other medico-legal complications which can flow from these procedures.

The MDOs assist with matters arising from clinical practice, whereas the BMA provides a service for disciplinary proceedings brought by an employer (such as a health trust) and arising from allegations of personal rather than professional misconduct.

For employed members (GP clinical assistants and hospital practitioners, for example) the distinction between *personal* and *professional* misconduct is not always readily apparent. The essential criterion is whether or not the allegations arise from specific episodes involving patient care. Each case is judged on its own merits. In 'mixed' situations, the MDO and the BMA will liaise and co-operate in the best interests of their mutual member.

In addition, Local Medical Committee (LMC) secretaries may be able to provide valuable, additional advice to GPs from a local viewpoint. Once again, MDOs will liaise and co-operate as necessary. Excellent working relationships between the MDOs and the BMA have been established over the years with both the old and the new NHS procedures.

The importance of seeking expert advice at an early stage of a complaint cannot be overemphasized. An apparently simple or 'trivial' complaint can, on occasions, develop into an expensive claim for damages or a serious allegation to the General Medical Council (GMC).

There is no earliest stage at which a member may seek advice from an MDO. The most effective advice is given *before* a problem has developed. From the pie chart (*see* Figure 12.1), it can be seen that a substantial number of doctors first make contact for help in avoiding a problem. This is often via the 24-hour, seven days a week telephone hotline.

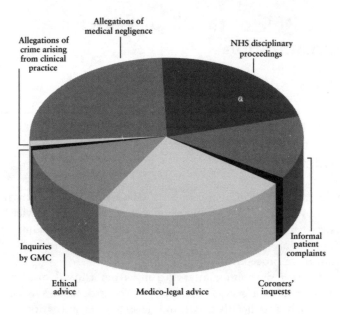

Figure 12.1:   Reasons why UK doctors contacted The MDU in 1995

Ethical advice in one-third of cases concerns medical confidentiality. An endless list of other problems arises, such as the possible consequences of removing a patient's name from the list, and the options open for alerting the proper authorities to the risk posed to patient care by an under-performing colleague.

Legal advice includes the interpretation of Acts of Parliament, the common law, NHS Executive circulars and the NHS Regulations, including the Terms of Service for GPs.

For complaints and disciplinary procedures, the following guidance will assist members to obtain the most effective advice.

Local resolution procedure ('in-house' or 'practice-based' complaints procedure)

The first stage of the NHS complaints procedure enables a complainant's concerns to be addressed with the minimum of delay. This also means that the respondent doctor has very little time to seek advice as necessary. In the first instance, the doctor may wish to telephone his or her MDO.

Often, after a fairly brief discussion, reassurance can be given that no clear pitfalls lie ahead. This is particularly important where concerns of a serious nature have been raised. An example might be where the doctor has been delayed and where the patient has died as a consequence of the delay – in the eyes of the complainant.

In practical terms, many local resolution cases involve an MDO to advise on issues peripheral to the substance of the complaint, such as confidentiality where a parent complains on behalf of a teenager under 16.

The vast majority of local resolution procedures will be satisfactorily resolved without formal assistance from an MDO. On some occasions, the MDO will help draft a written response, but only in very exceptional circumstances will a member of an MDO's staff attend a local resolution meeting with the complainant, as the doctor's representative.

Independent Review

Where a complaint proceeds to Independent Review, an MDO may wish to play a more active role. Most commonly this will involve the perusal of the documentation and advice on the written response. To enable the MDO to give adequate advice, the respondent should in the first instance provide photocopies of the following.

- The clinical records which *have been in the power or possession of the respondent doctor and which may* be relevant.
- The letter of complaint to the HA.
- A complete set of documents relating to the local resolution procedure.
- Covering correspondence with the HA/panel.
- A draft response suitable for submission to the HA.

Where appropriate, copies of the following should also be included.

- Correspondence with the Ombudsman.
- Correspondence with solicitors.
- Copies from appointment book, day book and/or visit request book.

- Statement of employed staff, e.g. receptionists, practice nurse, practice manager etc.

- Statement from telephone answering service.

- Statement from deputizing service.

- Statement from ambulance service.

- Statement of employed deputy, locum, registrar or assistant who is not a principal.

- Statement from HA employed staff, e.g. district nurse, casualty medical officer, consultant etc. – but only *with* the patient's consent.

- Hospital medical records – but only *with* the patient's consent.

- Press cuttings.

- Any other document which might be relevant.

In collecting evidence, the respondent doctor must take care to observe the basic rules of confidentiality. A doctor is entitled to a copy of all documentation which was at one time properly in the power and possession of that doctor. It is not open to a GP to ask for the hospital notes without the consent of the patient, although the GP is entitled to a discharge summary or letter arising from an admission whilst the patient was under that GP's care.

Given the non-disciplinary nature of Independent Review, the doctor will normally attend without representation. Only in exceptional circumstances will it be necessary for an MDO to send a representative to accompany the doctor, and it will be up to the discretion of the chairman of the panel whether the representative will be allowed to play an active role.

The Independent Review panel may ask the doctor why the Local Resolution Procedure failed and what steps the doctor proposes to improve the handling of any future complaint. Therefore, careful consideration must be given to the 'in-house' proceedings, even though the doctor may decide that the documentation relating to it will not be submitted as part of the written evidence to the panel.

The Ombudsman

The same rules concerning a request for assistance from an MDO apply to an investigation by the Ombudsman.

The Medical Discipline Committee

Where a GP is put on notice by a health authority that the disciplinary procedure is to be followed, the MDO should be contacted as soon as possible. All the documents described for Independent Review should be sent, and assistance is normally offered in preparing a reply in the first instance.

This reply may be different from the GP's response to the Independent Review panel because the issues in contention are likely to be more precise and may even ignore the main thrust of the patient's complaint upon which the disciplinary investigation is based. For example, the patient may have felt most aggrieved by the doctor's unsympathetic attitude, whereas the discipline committee may be more interested in the patient's description of apparent inadequate clinical management, perhaps mentioned as an aside by the patient.

GPs are entitled to full representation by an advocate at a disciplinary hearing, but such an advocate, according to the Regulations, cannot be a solicitor or barrister. MDOs can provide representatives who will all be very experienced with the old style Medical Service Committees. The MDU may provide either a full-time member of staff or someone from the panel of GP consultants, many of whom are or were LMC Secretaries.

The advocate will be entitled to present the GP's response to the case, cross-examine witnesses, and most difficult of all, sum up the GP's case at the end of the hearing. However, the advocate may not assist the respondent GP whilst he or she is being cross-examined by the health authority's representative (or 'prosecutor') or by members of the Committee.

Apart from providing expert advice and an advocate, an MDO will not pay any expenses incurred by the respondent GP, such as locum fees or travel costs (except in very rare cases where genuine hardship can be demonstrated), nor will an MDO pay any 'fine' imposed by the Discipline Committee.

FHS appeal

Where a GP is found in breach of the Terms of Service, an MDO will advise on the likely success of an appeal to the FHS Appeal Authority which for England is based in Harrogate. In some cases, an expert opinion may be sought in advance of a hearing from an experienced GP in clinical practice, or from a lawyer, depending on the precise circumstances.

Where an appeal hearing is held, the doctor will normally be accompanied by a representative (non-legally qualified advocate) of the MDO, but the regulations do allow for a solicitor. In a small number of cases one will be instructed on behalf of the GP. Such a decision is at the discretion of the MDO and is likely to depend on the nature of the appeal (i.e. if the grounds for appeal rest on legal or clinical arguments) rather than the complexity or seriousness of the complaint and its potential for a further referral to the GMC or a subsequent claim for damages in a civil court of law.

The NHS Tribunal

The NHS Tribunal is the most serious disciplinary procedure which can be brought against a GP by the NHS. The purpose of the NHS Tribunal is to determine if the GP's name should remain on the list of a HA, or whether the continued inclusion is prejudicial to the effective provision of general medical services. It is very rarely held.

NHS Tribunals are conducted on a formal legal basis. Evidence is given under oath and doctors may be represented by a lawyer, usually a barrister instructed by the MDO. The standard of proof is higher than applies to any of the foregoing procedures. In other words the tribunal must be satisfied that the facts of the case are established *beyond reasonable doubt*, as against *on the balance of probability* (i.e. more likely than not). This high standard of proof is similar to that required by the GMC and the criminal courts.

Where a doctor is advised that he or she will be subjected to the NHS Tribunal procedure, assistance from an MDO should be sought at the earliest opportunity to enable instructions to be given to lawyers to draft a defence.

The General Medical Council

Where a doctor has been found in breach of the Terms of Service by a Medical Discipline Committee and a large recovery of remuneration recommended, or where other circumstances of the case which might fall outside the Terms of Service such as a breach of confidentiality suggest possible serious professional misconduct, the case might be referred to the GMC. This may occur at any stage of proceedings and from any source. The complaining patient may alert the GMC on day one, or the HA, the Ombudsman or the Appeal Authority at a later stage.

Receipt of a GMC's initial letter asking for comments must be acknowledged in person by the doctor, but no attempt should be made by the doctor to give an explanation without expert assistance. In preparing the formal response, even in apparently 'trivial' cases the doctor is normally assisted either by a member of the MDO's staff or by a solicitor, with or without advice from a barrister.

Assistance before the Overseas Committee of the GMC with respect to criteria for full registration is normally provided by a non-lawyer advocate on the staff of an MDO.

Litigation

In about 6% of complaints made to a HA, the patient or patient representative will subsequently threaten legal proceedings through the civil courts for compensation. In many of these cases the complaints procedure will have been used as a 'dry run' to test the merits of a claim. The first step in litigation is normally a *letter before action* from the patient's solicitor asking for disclosure of the clinical records. A copy of this letter should be sent to an MDO together with the entirety of the original clinical records by recorded delivery. Acknowledgement of receipt of the letter must be made before action can be undertaken by the MDO staff. There is usually no necessity for the doctor to communicate directly with the patient's solicitors at any stage.

Summary

1   Seek expert advice early.

2   Provide advisers with a *full* set of documents.

As a very rough guide, the level of assistance shown in the table on the following page can be expected.

| | Nature of advice | | Type of representation | | | | |
| | | | | Advocate | | | |
	Telephone advice	Written advice	'Silent friend'	Non-lawyer advocate	Solicitor	'Junior' barrister	QC
In-house	✓✓	✓					
Independent Review	✓✓	✓✓		×	×	×	×
Ombudsman	✓✓	✓✓		×	×	×	×
Disciplinary Committee	✓✓	✓	✓	✓✓	×	×	×
Disciplinary Appeal	✓✓	✓		✓✓	✓	✓✓	✓✓
NHS Tribunal	✓✓	✓	×	×	✓	✓✓	✓✓
Criminal charges	✓✓	✓	×	×	✓	✓✓	✓✓
GMC – Preliminary screener	✓✓	✓		✓✓	✓		
GMC – Preliminary Proceedings Committee	✓	✓			✓✓		
GMC – Professional Conduct Committee		✓			✓	✓✓	✓
GMC – Appeal to Privy Council			×	×	✓	✓	✓✓
GMC – Health Committee	✓✓	✓	✓✓		✓✓	✓	✓✓
GMC – Performance Review	✓✓	✓	×	×	✓		
Coroner's Court	✓✓	✓		×	✓✓	✓	
Misuse of Drugs Tribunal	✓	✓			✓	✓	

✓ = common ✓✓ = most common × = proscribed

13 Complaints and the Legal System

Gerard Panting

A single clinical incident may give rise to a number of legal consequences. The prescription of a beta blocker to a known asthmatic
resulting in an acute asthma attack and death, is likely to lead to a
complaint which may progress to Independent Review. Disciplinary
proceedings may follow. The health authority/health board may refer the
doctor to the General Medical Council (GMC) and/or the NHS
Tribunal. During the complaints procedure, the Health Service Commissioner or Ombudsman may also become involved. Simultaneously, the
Coroner (in England, Wales and Northern Ireland) or Procurator Fiscal
in Scotland will conduct his own investigation into the death which may
result in the papers being referred to the Director of Public Prosecutions
who must decide whether or not the doctor should be prosecuted for
manslaughter. In addition, a claim in medical negligence may be made
against the doctor.

The written record of a complaints procedure is a disclosable document
in any subsequent legal proceedings. It is vital therefore that the facts are
fully established before any attempt is made to explain events to the
complainant. Inaccuracies and factual errors will be a severe embarrass-
ment to the defence. Fear of admitting liability deters many doctors from
apologizing for errors properly established; there is no point in attempting
to deny the self-evident. It is prudent to seek independent advice before
making a reply to a substantive complaint.

Establishing the facts

Each investigation has its own purpose but common to all is the need to
establish the facts, a process which becomes increasingly difficult the
longer the time between the events in question and the investigation. Even
where there is broad agreement on what took place, there is likely to be
some disagreement over points of detail, some of which may be central to
the final determination of the case.

Where there is a dispute as to the facts, a court or tribunal will have to
decide which version of events is to be preferred on the balance of

probability. Witnesses of fact may be called – friends and relations who were involved in the patient's care, some of whom may claim that their memory of events is impeccable. The defendant doctor too may be able to call witnesses such as district nurses and other doctors who attended the patient but often there is no one else involved and the defence must rely on the doctor's own testimony and contemporaneous notes. If the notes are inadequate, an otherwise defensible case may result in a finding against the doctor.

An adequate medical record is one that enables the doctor to reconstruct the consultation without relying on memory. Details of the presenting symptoms, answers to direct questions, findings on examination (including negative findings such as 'abdo ✓'), the clinical impression formed, the treatment prescribed and further management advised, including follow-up arrangements should all be recorded. A high standard of notekeeping will be assumed to go hand in hand with a high standard of practice. Equally, shoddy notes will be equated with shoddy practice. Practice diaries and call books may also prove important as may the clinical information recorded on pathology request forms. Many cases involve out-of-hours calls and where these are dealt with by telephone advice alone, it is common practice for no record to be kept at all. The patient and/or his relatives may give a detailed account of the conversation. If the doctor cannot remember receiving the telephone call, let alone what was said, the plaintiff's statement is likely to be accepted. Only if the doctor keeps a bound exercise book by the telephone and records details of all calls and the advice given can he hope to refute inaccurate assertions by the patient or his representatives. The importance to the defence in any proceedings of comprehensive, contemporaneous records cannot be overstated.

Medical negligence

To succeed in a medical negligence action, the plaintiff must prove three points: first, that the doctor owed a duty of care to the patient. Second, that the doctor breached that duty of care and third, that the patient suffered harm as a result of the breach of duty of care.

There is rarely a dispute over the existence of a duty of care, as the duty is established as soon as the doctor offers advice or assistance, even in informal surroundings. In addition, the Terms of Service defines a doctor's patients as persons accepted on to his own list or on the list of any doctors for whom he is deputizing, patients accepted as temporary residents and persons to whom the doctor may be requested to give treatment which is immediately required owing to accident or other emergency at any place in his practice area provided that he is available to provide such treatment.

Only where the doctor acts as an independent medical assessor for a third party, such as a company doctor reporting on fitness for employment, is the presence of a duty of care open to question.

Far more difficult is determining whether or not the doctor fulfilled the duty of care. The test applied in civil courts in England and Wales is the Bolam test (a similar standard is applied in courts in Scotland and Northern Ireland). Bolam sued the Management Committee for Barnet Hospital after his leg was broken during electroconvulsive therapy. He claimed that the failure to administer a muscle relaxant prior to treatment was negligent. Both plaintiff and defendant called expert evidence, the plaintiff expert maintained that the administration of a muscle relaxant was mandatory while those for the defendant stated that it was not. Faced with conflicting expert medical evidence, the judge, Mr Justice McNair ruled that '*a doctor is not guilty of negligence if acting in accordance with a practice accepted as proper by a responsible body of medical opinion skilled in that particular art, even though a body of adverse opinion also exists amongst medical men*', putting it the other way round, a doctor is not negligent if he is acting in accordance with such a practice merely because there is a body of opinion which takes a contrary view. In other words, a doctor will be able to defend his or her actions if able to call upon experts to testify that what he or she did was reasonable in the circumstances.

At first blush, defence of a medical negligence claim appears simple – just find an expert who will say that the defendant doctor acted reasonably and the defence is home and dry. But for the defence to succeed, the expert's opinion must be sustainable in the face of rigorous cross-examination and the court must be satisfied that the facts upon which the expert opinion was based are correct. As each part of the case is raked over in fine detail, it becomes apparent that passing the Bolam test in practice requires a high standard of care.

Compensation is awarded in medical negligence claims for damage that would have been avoided but for the negligence of the doctor (or his staff). It is not enough for the plaintiff to say that the care provided was substandard and that the result is poor, the causal link must be proved. Complaints and disciplinary procedures are not concerned with outcome but in claims outcome is all important – if the patient came to no harm despite appalling care, no compensation is payable.

Litigation

Litigation is a long-winded and risky business. The plaintiff requires perseverance, patience and money. Legal aid is available for medical negligence cases provided that the claimant qualifies. For those that do not, the level of legal costs is a considerable deterrent.

As Lord Woolf noted in his report on the civil justice system in England and Wales, *Access to Justice*, the current system has numerous defects: it is too expensive; too slow; there is inequality of resources between the plaintiffs and defendants; it is too unpredictable and the adversarial nature of litigation results in cases being run by the parties with the rules of court frequently ignored and unenforced.

Each claim turns on its own set of facts so the first port of call for the plaintiff's solicitor will be the holders of the relevant records, who may also be the potential defendants. Disclosure is usually granted voluntarily as there are a variety of means open to the plaintiff to force discovery, merely protracting proceedings and incurring unnecessary costs for all concerned. Furthermore, disclosure allows the complainant to obtain independent medical advice on the merits of the claim, following which the majority of claims are discontinued.

If the claim is pursued, it will progress as follows (the system in operation in Northern Ireland and Scotland has broadly similar procedural steps but differs in some respects). The plaintiff issues and serves proceedings (County Court Summons/High Court Writ) naming the plaintiff(s) and defendant(s). The full details of the claim may be attached or served separately weeks or months later in the Particular of Claim (County Court) or Statement of Claim (High Court). Medical reports on current condition and prognosis should also be attached. In response to the Writ or Summons, the defendant (usually via a solicitor) files an Acknowledgement of Service: failure to do so within 21 days (County Court) or 14 days (High Court) may result in the plaintiff entering judgment against the defendant which it may not be possible to set aside. Consequently, a Writ or Summons should be regarded as a legal emergency.

Once the Particulars of Claim or Statement of Claim setting out full details is served, each defendant must file an equally detailed defence. The two sides can now ask each other for further and better particulars of their respective cases albeit some of the answers received are less helpful than others.

Once this cross-interrogation is complete, pleadings are said to be closed and an 'Order for Directions' is made setting out a timetable for exchange of witness and expert statements in preparation for trial.

Very few cases (less than 2%) come to trial, the rest being settled or abandoned en route. A handful of cases where liability is not in dispute and quantum of damages cannot be agreed result in the case being tried on quantum alone. All settlements involving minors require approval of the court, a process which can attract some publicity.

At trial the main evidence of each witness is given in statement form and any appearance in the witness box is limited to cross-examination by the opposing side and a brief re-examination by the side calling the witness. Witness statements are usually prepared in rough form prior to the service of the defence and refined immediately prior to exchange.

There are no juries in medical negligence cases. The judge must consider the evidence, resolving any disputes of fact on a balance of probabilities. Judgement may be given at the conclusion of the case (ex tempore) or deferred to a later date.

The question of costs is considered next. Costs follow the cause, i.e. the loser pays all. However, there is usually considerable legal wrangling over how much the victorious side's costs should be and as a rule of thumb the victor can expect to recover two-thirds of his/her legal expenditure. In general, a costs award against a legally aided plaintiff cannot be enforced without the leave of the court which in reality will only occur if the plaintiff comes into money.

Proposed changes in England and Wales

Lord Woolf's report *Access to Justice* proposes considerable changes to the civil justice system in England and Wales. His proposals include encouraging people to treat litigation as a last resort with an emphasis on other methods of resolving disputes such as offering a full explanation at an early stage or using alternative dispute resolution, for example mediation before or during legal proceedings. Where litigation ensues, he suggests three 'tracks': an expanded small claims jurisdiction with a financial limit of £3 000: a fast-track for straightforward cases up to £10 000 in value with limited procedures and fixed timetables and costs, and finally multi-track for cases of more than £10 000 in value in which the timetable will be managed by the courts. It is likely that the majority of medical negligence cases would be allocated to the multi-track.

Lord Woolf lists the essential elements for case management by the courts as follows: allocation of each case to the track and court at which it can be dealt with most appropriately; encouraging and assisting the parties to settle cases, or at least to agree on the particular issues; encouraging the use of alternative dispute resolution; identifying at an early stage the key issues which need full trial and summarily disposing of weak cases and hopeless issues; achieving transparency and control of costs; increasing the client's knowledge of what the progress and costs of the case would involve, and fixing and enforcing a strict timetable of procedural steps leading to trial and for trial itself.

The report devotes a chapter to medical negligence. Although he makes a number of specific recommendations such as pre-litigation protocols in medical negligence cases and the introduction of a specialist list of judges with special experience and expertise to ensure that such cases are dealt with efficiently, his proposals if accepted will follow the general scheme set out above. Lord Woolf proposes special training for judges appointed to the medical negligence list.

Lord Woolf's recommendations, if implemented, will have a considerable impact on the management of medical negligence cases.

Providing a full and clear explanation combined with an apology where appropriate is an integral part of the new NHS complaints system and so should already be in place. Even where this fails to resolve the issue, any differences between the complainant and respondent doctor should at least be more defined as a result.

The introduction of alternative dispute resolution (ADR), particularly mediation, will require a different approach from doctors and their advisers as well as patients. Mediation has been highly successful in resolving commercial disputes and has the advantage that it offers the chance of resolving differences between the parties rather than just extracting financial compensation.

Should a case proceed further, a pre-litigation protocol will allow a short time for the defence to consider the claim and issue a detailed response. To comply with the protocol, potential claims must be investigated urgently which will usually involve a meeting between the doctor and his advisers followed by a swift assessment, where necessary by reference to experts.

Should a case proceed to litigation, a strict timetable will be laid down. Failure to abide by the time limits is likely to result in a judgement against the doctor, so again speed will be of the essence.

Damages

Financial compensation is intended, insofar as money can, to restore the patient's position to that he or she would have been in had the injury never occurred. General damages are awarded for pain, suffering and loss of amenity and special damages for particular items of monetary loss such as loss of earnings, necessary modifications to the home or any other specific item of expenditure necessitated by the injury. In addition, interest is payable on general damages from the date of service of proceedings and on special damages from the date of the accident although no interest is payable on compensation for future losses.

Cases which proceed

Potential plaintiffs may pursue medical negligence claims from a variety of motives. Obtaining financial compensation is important to patients who have suffered substantial financial loss, or who are no longer able to work and parents of severely handicapped children are able to secure their child's future by obtaining a large financial award. Others may pursue a claim out of a sense of grievance or because they feel they cannot uncover the true facts by any other means or in an attempt to make a point in the hope that similar cases can be avoided in the future. A small minority of claims amount to an attempt to cash in on alleged medical negligence.

Providing a full and sympathetic explanation to potential litigants will go someway to satisfying their needs and may even dissuade some from pursuing a claim but for those whose lives have undergone dramatic change as a result of personal tragedy, financial compensation will remain the priority.

In the latter category are the various causes of severe handicap in childhood: delayed diagnosis of meningitis or dehydration associated with gastroenteritis and failure to arrange appropriate tests for a mother at high risk of having a Down's syndrome child. If harm is demonstrated to have resulted from negligence in any of these cases, the award will be calculated on the basis of providing for all the extra requirements of that child for the rest of his or her life.

The loss of a parent may also result in a large claim. Negligence resulting in the death of a breadwinner with 20 years of life remaining will be calculated on the basis of what that individual would have earned during the period discounted because the payment is made as a one-off lump sum.

Death of a non-earning mother may necessitate the employment of a nanny and/or housekeeper to take on her responsibilities – the cost will have been calculated as special damages.

Delayed diagnosis of subacute bacterial endocarditis resulting in cerebral emboli in a 35-year-old patient may mean that patient will not be able to work again: damages will include compensation for loss of earnings until retirement.

Where there is no requirement for continuing care, damages will be of a much lower order. The death of a child may attract only bereavement damages of £7 500; subcutaneous fat atrophy following a steroid injection several thousand pounds; the prescription of a drug to a patient known to be allergic resulting in a mild reaction a few hundred pounds.

Conclusion

Doctors are accountable for their acts and omissions to a number of courts and tribunals. Whilst the burden of proof lies with the complainant, plaintiff or prosecutor, the doctor will be required to produce evidence to corroborate his own account of what happened to justify his actions. Clear comprehensive, contemporaneous records will always be the cornerstone of the defence, their absence would inevitably prejudice the outcome for the doctor.

14 How to Avoid Complaints and How to Respond to Them

Tony Stanton

Complaints have been defined as expressions of dissatisfaction which require a response. With such a broad definition it would clearly never be possible to avoid complaints, but by looking at some of the commoner reasons which give rise to complaints, it should at least prove possible to contain them, to reduce their numbers and to try to prevent them recurring.

An ABC of how to minimize the risk of a complaint can be grouped under three headings:

1 attitude

2 be prepared

3 care.

Attitude was very commonly identified by people making complaints under the old Service Committee procedures, and since attitude of itself was not defined in the terms of service there was a lot of frustration and confusion when the patients found that they could not effectively take their complaints any further. Comments such as 'It's the attitude of that receptionist that gets me' or 'the attitude of the doctor when I asked for a certificate was unbelievable!', are often heard on the proverbial omnibus.

Improving attitudes is hard work. It involves looking at how the practice functions and seeing how best to improve access. A check list should include looking at the following key areas.

- Can the telephone system cope? How long does it take someone to get through? Have the staff had telephone answering training?

- Appointments – are they designed for the convenience of patients or doctors? Are there enough slots for urgent cases? What about babies and young children with worried parents?

- Do the doctors lead by example? Or is a receptionist who tries to help an anxious patient subsequently criticized by the doctor and puts up a barricade in future?

- Have the doctors ever looked at their consultation techniques?

- What about patient attitudes? Is there a patient support group which can help?

A system involving a patients' complaint committee, made up of members from a patient participation group, has been described by Dr Pietroni and Sybilla de Uray-Ura, the patient liaison worker at the Marylebone Health Centre. This was a two-way process, which considered complaints made by patients and complaints made by staff about patients. The two-way process of the procedure ensured the patients received quick response to complaints and helped morale of the practice staff.

Attitudes are inevitably reflected in behaviour, and the best way to look at this is to be prepared. Two good approaches to this are:

1   having a clear practice charter

2   developing an incident reporting system.

Patient charters have tended to be regarded with considerable suspicion by many GPs who have felt that raising patient expectations without providing adequate resources is a recipe for mutual assured dissatisfaction. However, since GPs have a Terms of Service obligation to provide practice leaflets and written information about their complaints procedures, these can be incorporated in a practice charter which meets the philosophy of the individual practice and which provides an ideal opportunity to set out in plain English both patients' rights and patients' responsibilities.

It also helps to be prepared by developing an incident reporting system. An example of this is given in the NHS Executive booklet *Practice-based Complaints Procedures* and is a simple reporting form on which anyone in the practice can note details of a patient contact which they feel to have been less than satisfactory, and for that report to be passed to the practice complaints administrator. Examples might include dissatisfaction at the reception desk or a consultation where the doctor or practice nurse feels that not everything went as well as might have been expected. In such situations the practice complaints administrator could then contact the patient concerned and give them a chance to express any unhappiness without waiting for an actual complaint to be generated.

Last but not least, in an ABC of avoiding complaints, is care. A practice which is perceived as doing its best to care for patients will generate far fewer complaints than those perceived as being uncaring. Care includes the following.

- Listening to patients – what is the patient actually trying to say?

- Carefully examining the patient.

- Keeping effective records, including important negative findings.

- Keeping an open mind – anxious patients can develop physical illnesses.

- Review the diagnosis – people who keep coming back, especially if they are accompanied by a relative or friend expressing concern, often benefit from a fresh look at their condition.

- Have you explained your findings and thinking to the patient?

- Is the prescription necessary? Is it safe? Are the instructions clear?

- Can you charge for that certificate? If in doubt, do not.

- You promise to refer for a consultant opinion or specialist investigation – have you done so? Do you have a fail-safe system?

- How do you tell patients about the results of their test or hospital referral?

- When a patient dies do you have simple and sympathetic arrangements for completing the death certificate and explaining medical terminology?

- If a patient who you have been looking after unexpectedly deteriorates, and is seriously ill in hospital or unexpectedly dies, do you contact the family to talk through the difficulties of the diagnosis, to offer an explanation and an apology if one is due?

In reviewing the care of patients which has given rise to reasons for serious complaints, do remember that the most common reason for complaint is delay. ·

- Delay in diagnosis.

- Delay in referring.

- Delay in visiting.

Keeping accurate and complete records helps to minimize the risk of a complaint by:

- encouraging the doctor to re-evaluate the situation
- ensuring good communication with other team members who may need to access the records
- avoiding the additional charge of poor record-keeping.

The Medical Defence Union advises GPs to make an entry in the medical record after every:

- consultation
- visit
- telephone conversation
- out-of-hours communication
- prescription issued.

Despite all these precautions complaints will inevitably arise. When they do, and when they have been investigated, explained and apologized for if necessary, take the opportunity to learn any lessons and to review systems within the practice.

Appendix

Framework for a practice charter

We are committed to giving you the best possible service. This will be achieved by working together. Help us to help you.
Please read this leaflet carefully. It will help you to get the best out of the service we offer.

Our responsibilities to you
You will be treated as an individual in the care and attention you receive and will be given courtesy and respect.

Your responsibilities to us
We ask that you treat the doctors, or practice staff and their families with the same courtesy and respect.

Our responsibilities to you
Following discussion you will receive the most appropriate care, and this will be given by suitably qualified people. No care or treatment will be given without your consent.

Your responsibilities to us
In return do please try to follow the medical advice offered, and to take any medication as advised. If in doubt, please ask.

Our responsibilities to you
You have the right to see your health records, and we shall do our best to keep these confidential. The health authority does have the right to ask us to return your medical records to them at any time.

Your responsibilities to us
If there is anything you do not want entered in your medical records, please make sure you tell us. If you become aware of any incorrect information, again please do let us know.

Our responsibilities to you
The team of people in the practice involved in your care is quite large – the people looking after you will give you their names and how you can contact them.

Your responsibilities to us
If you change your name or address, please let us know straight away.

Our responsibilities to you
It is our job to give you treatment and advice. Normally we do this at the surgery. We provide an appointment system (give details)/walk in surgery sessions (give details). We will try to ensure that you are seen on time but some consultations take longer than others and we have no way of knowing about this in advance. If there is a long delay, an explanation will be given by the receptionist.

Your responsibilities to us
Please do everything you can to keep appointments, and tell us as soon as possible if you cannot. Please try to be punctual – if you arrive late, this may cause delays and inconvenience to other patients. Please let the receptionist know when you arrive at the surgery. If your problem is an urgent one, please do make that clear to the receptionist.

Our responsibilities to you
It is our responsibility to decide whether, when and where you should be seen. To help us do this, we have trained staff who will need to ask you some straightforward questions. These are designed to help and not to obstruct.

Your responsibilities to us
Please do not ask for a home visit unless the patient cannot be brought to the surgery. Most young children who are unwell and running a temperature can quite safely be brought to the surgery. If you do need a home visit, please try to let us know before (give time).

Our responsibilities to you
We provide cover for emergencies at all times. (Give details of telephone answering arrangements including out of hours.) Your call will result in:

- advice, which may include waiting for the next surgery

- an urgent consultation at the surgery

- an urgent consultation at our out-of-hours centre (give details)

- a home visit if medically required

- immediate referral to hospital.

Your responsibilities to us
Please do not call out of hours, unless about an emergency which cannot wait until the next surgery. Please remember that your doctors need rest and relaxation, just like everyone else. If you do need to telephone us, please have a pen and paper handy to note details of any advice you are given. If you are in any doubt, or if there is any change, please telephone us back.

Our responsibilities to you
We want to improve services, and we will therefore welcome any comments or suggestions you have. We operate a practice-based complaints procedure, and if you are not happy with any service you have received from us, please let us know. If you do have a complaint please contact (give name/job title and deputy). We shall do our best to:

- acknowledge your complaint normally within two working days

- investigate it properly and in confidence
- provide you with a written summary normally within ten working days.

Your responsibilities to us
You have the right at any time to leave our list and to register with another practice. We also have the right to have patients removed from our list, but in general this is only done when the doctor/patient relationship has broken down. We will remove from our list immediately patients who are violent or seriously abusive to any of the practice staff.

Help us to help you
If you have good ideas about ways of improving things that those of us in the practice are too close to the work to see for ourselves, please let us know. We value your comments and suggestions.

Index